To Josen

a small token of thanks
for all your help and
encouragement. The
pregnancy was long and the
outcome uncertain — but the
midwifery was absolutely
first class throughout!

D1334496

June 1996

VERDI
AND HIS
OPERAS

For Francesca and Imogen,
Lawrence and Robert,
Daniel and Bevan.

The World of Opera

Verdi

by Robert Hardcastle

Spellmount

Staplehurst

British Library Cataloguing in
Publication Data:
A catalogue record for this book is
available from the British Library

ISBN 1-873376-61-8

First published in the UK in 1996 by
Spellmount Limited,
The Old Rectory, Staplehurst,
Kent TN12 0AZ
1 3 5 7 9 8 6 4 2

Edited and designed by
Three's Company,
5 Dryden Street,
London WC2

Printed and bound in Great Britain by
Butler & Tanner Ltd, Frome and London

Contents

Author's Note

A considerable debt to my predecessors will, I hope, be apparent from the acknowledgements in the text and in the brief bibliography that follows. Scholars and general readers alike owe much to an early champion of Verdi's cause, the remarkable Franz Werfel – third husband of Alma Mahler, author of *The Song of Bernadette* and of *Verdi: A Novel of the Opera* – and to a previous generation of writers such as Ferruccio Bonavia, Edward J. Dent, Dyneley Hussey and Francis Toye, all of whom worked at a time when Verdi's reputation was still under a cloud and when many of his earlier operas were rarely, if ever, performed.

The situation today could hardly be more different. All the operas are accessible, if not always in live performance then certainly on radio, on disc and, increasingly, on videotape. The seemingly limitless resources of the huge Verdi archive continue to inspire and to deepen the understanding of many contemporary writers, of whom Julian Budden must receive special mention. His three volumes on *The Operas of Verdi* stand as one of the great monuments of modern musical criticism.

I am equipped neither by training nor by temperament to add to such formidable scholarship. My aim has been much more modest: to offer a reasonably up-to-date commentary to the general reader who wishes to know more about the man and his music, and the world in which he lived and worked. Even as I write these words, part of that world has gone up in flames at La Fenice in Venice, where five of Verdi's operas, including *La Traviata* and *Rigoletto*, were first performed. It is much to be hoped that, true to its name, this great opera house will rise from the ashes to serve future generations of composers, performers and opera-lovers.

I should like to record my sincere thanks to George Lloyd who, despite a busy schedule that would daunt many a younger composer, took time out to contribute a Foreword to this book. My indebtedness also extends to a group of loyal and long-suffering friends whose advice, at various points along the way, I have sought and often taken. Among them are Peter Lymbery, John Spare, David Inman, Ray Burford and, in particular, my colleague and fellow-writer John Walton, who has not only guided my steps throughout but who also allowed me to borrow his word-processor when my own collapsed under the strain. One cannot ask more of a friend than that.

For their encouragement and support I should also like to thank various members of my family, including Dr John Payne for his guidance on medical matters, and my daughter-in-law Rachael for her help in preparing an index and checking proofs. Indeed, to all those who have helped in bringing my work to press I record my gratitude: any errors, inconsistencies and other infelicities that persist are entirely my own work, not theirs.

Robert Hardcastle
Royal Tunbridge Wells: 1996

Foreword

When I was a student in the thirties critical opinion still maintained that Verdi was not a composer to be taken seriously, even though the general public had loved his operas since the middle of the nineteenth century. Despite Verdi's enormous popularity, even in England, his music was written off as only fit for street barrel organs. I was on the side of the public – and I knew exactly why. Verdi's early and middle operas had a drive, a vitality and an eruptive quality that can only be compared to middle-period Beethoven. His tunes could sweep you along: but then they were tunes that always fitted the character and the situation on the stage, for Verdi had a wonderful dramatic sense. Even when he had grown out of music written for virtuoso vocal performance, his florid *cabalettas* were always to the point.

For me, *Rigoletto* remains as near to the ideal opera as is possible: the balance between the stage action, the singers and the orchestra is perfect. Historically, composers have always swung from one to another of these three components of opera. By the time Verdi wrote *Otello* the swing was away from the supremacy of the singer – a process that has continued to this day.

But Verdi has gained as well as lost. In his later operas the dramatic content had become more intense, the role of the orchestra more important. In the last act of *Otello* the poignancy of the vocal line, the orchestral colour and the drama have become so powerful that even today, after knowing the score since I was a boy, only very rarely can I bring myself to listen to it.

In spite of my love for Verdi's music and my admiration for the man himself, I probably knew only about half of what was there. Much more is now known about Verdi and his music than was known a couple of generations ago: all his lesser known works, and some that had completely vanished, are now being performed. Research has brought to light facets of his character not previously known.

Robert Hardcastle is fortunate to have so much of this information at his disposal: he has thus been enabled to write a new and vivid life of Giuseppe Verdi which comes just at the right time, and I hope it will fascinate the general reader as much as it has fascinated me.

George Lloyd
London, 1995

Chapter 1

'Bravo, Bravo, Viva Il Maestro!'

The baptismal entry in the register of the parish church at Le Roncole is in Latin, in accordance with normal practice. But French is the language used in the municipal records, where Verdi's forenames are shown as Joseph Fortunin François.

During the month of February 1842 the Teatro alla Scala in Milan echoed and re-echoed to the sound of builders carrying out a major refit in the famous old opera house. The auditorium was full of noise and dust as carpenters, masons and other craftsmen went about their various tasks. On stage and among the orchestra it was business as usual, for a full rehearsal was under way. Not even building works could be allowed to disturb the normal production schedule. But the singers and the musicians were disturbed, very much so. The orchestra replied to the off-stage bangs and crashes by playing as loudly as possible, ignoring all the dynamic markings on the parts in front of them. Disgruntled soloists showed their disapproval by throwing more tantrums than usual, and the chorus sang as badly as they knew how. From the podium a tall, impressive young man tried to make sense from the musical chaos around him. Let him take up the story in his own words:

A bust of the composer now stands in the fore-court of his birthplace at Le Roncole.

Presently the chorus started to sing, as carelessly as before, the *Va, pensiero*, but before they got through half a dozen bars the theatre was as quiet as a church. The men had stopped working, one by one, and there they were sitting about on the ladders and scaffolding, listening! When the number was finished, they broke out into the noisiest applause I have ever heard, crying, *Bravo, bravo, viva il maestro*! and beating on the woodwork with their tools. It was at that moment I knew what the future had in store for me.

His unfailing theatrical instinct told Giuseppe Verdi that, at long last, he had a success on his hands. The work he had been rehearsing under such impossible conditions we know as *Nabucco* – originally *Nabucodonosor* – an opera composed to a text by Temistocle Solera, a Milanese poet and librettist. Its first performance on 9 March 1842, a few days after the rehearsal, proved to be a great triumph. At twenty-eight years of age Verdi had arrived, after a long and eventful journey: a journey as dramatic and as full of tragedy as the many operas to follow in the years ahead.

Verdi was born in 1813, the same year as Richard Wagner, in the hamlet of Le Roncole in the Duchy of Parma. Nearby is the attractive small town of Busseto, the seat of the Pallavicini family. Parma, bounded by the River

Po to the north and the Apennines to the south, was one of the many duchies, republics and minor kingdoms which together with the Papal States divided the whole of the Italian peninsula. The occupying armies of Napoleon Bonaparte had imposed some semblance of unity, but his power had been broken earlier that year by defeat of the French and their allies at the battle of Leipzig.

Verdi was less than a year old when the Austrians and a villainous collection of mercenaries started to drive the French out of northern Italy, plundering and pillaging as they went. As is the way with most victorious armies they made little distinction between friend and foe, so that local inhabitants caught up in the path of their advance were as much at risk as the enemy they were pursuing.

Against this hazardous background is set the first of a number of dramatic scenes in Verdi's life which seem to embrace fact and fantasy in equal measure. According to Giuseppina Strepponi, the celebrated soprano who became Verdi's second wife, when a group of rampaging soldiers reached Le Roncole his mother saved herself and her child by climbing the belfry of the village church of Madonna dei Prati, to remain in hiding there while murder, rape and pillage went on below.

Verdi himself believed this story to be true, but his testimony in such matters cannot always be relied upon. As an old man he made much of his lowly origins, telling his French biographer Camille Bellaigue that 'he had a hard time as a boy'. He used to say that he had been born poor in a poor village. 'I had no way to teach myself anything. They put a miserable spinet into my hands, and some time later I began to write notes . . . notes upon notes . . . that is all!'

But photographs of his birthplace show a simple, two-storied brick-and-timber building typical of the region, with shuttered windows and a long, sloping roof enclosing a stable on one side. Not the house of a successful merchant or powerful local landowner, certainly, but neither is it the 'wretched habitation' described by some of the composer's many biographers. Now preserved as a national museum, the house stands in its own courtyard, with a few trees and shrubs to provide much-needed shade in the long summer months. The Verdi household was in fact a centre of village life, for it served as the local village store and tavern, where farmers could make their modest purchases, exchange gossip and relax over a drink at the end of their working day.

As proprietor of such an establishment Verdi's father was not really a member of the peasantry, neither was he completely illiterate as has sometimes been suggested. He came from a long line of traders, inn-keepers and small landowners. When his son had made enough money to buy property in the area, he often bought back land that had once belonged to his forefathers.

Verdi's mother, whose maiden name was Luigia Uttini, and who could trace her ancestry back to Alessandro and Domenico Scarlatti, came from a similar background. Her family, in which we are told 'there was a great deal of music', had kept a tavern for many years in the small village of Saliceto di Cadeo, just west of Busseto. She and Carlo Verdi were married in 1805. There were two children, Giuseppe and a younger sister, Giuseppa Francesca, who contracted meningitis as an infant and died at the age of seventeen.

Antonio Barezzi, a successful merchant in Busseto, was Verdi's greatest benefactor and became, in the composer's own words, a 'second father' to him.

'They put a miserable spinet into my hands,' said Verdi. What peasant family could have bought a spinet, however miserable, for a musically-gifted child? It is true that at that time there were a number of second-hand instruments to be had, selling at modest prices as people traded them in to buy or hire pianofortes, which were then coming into fashion. However, if Verdi's family had really been as poor as he made them out to be, even a well-used second-hand spinet would probably have been beyond their reach.

What is certain is that his father, impressed by the boy's love of music and his burgeoning talent, bought a spinet for him when he was eight years old. Verdi's true feelings may be judged by the fact that it never left his side: he treasured the instrument all his life. Now it stands in the museum of La Scala in Milan, and under the lid can still be seen a label that bears touching testimony to the skill of the young musician:

These hammers were repaired and re-covered by me, Stefano Cavaletti, and I fitted the pedals which I presented: I also repaired the said hammers gratuitously, seeing the good disposition the young Verdi has for learning to play this instrument, which is sufficient for my complete satisfaction –
Anno Domini 1821

Verdi's rudimentary musical education during his early years was provided by the organist at Le Roncole, Pietro Baistrocchi. The village priest taught him to read and write, and he served as an acolyte in the local church. On one occasion he was so caught up in the music from the organ that he forgot his liturgical duties, until a powerful nudge from the priest sent him sprawling down the altar steps.

Before he reached the age of ten both teachers had died, and the *maestrino* earned a degree of fame in and around Le Roncole by taking on some of the duties of local organist. But by this time Carlo Verdi had come to the conclusion that his son needed a broader and more rigorous education than could be found in the village. He arranged with a cobbler friend in Busseto to have the boy taken in as a week-day lodger to make it possible for him to attend the local *ginnasio*, or grammar school. On Sundays and feast days he walked the three or four miles back to Le Roncole where, at the age of twelve, he was formally appointed church organist on a token salary.

These facts are well known and well documented. But there are other stories about the young Verdi at this time which may or may not be true. We are told, for example, that he carried his boots around his neck to save unnecessary wear. Also, that after setting out one Christmas morning, well before daybreak, he missed his footing on the winding road, fell into a deep dyke running alongside filled with water after recent heavy rain, and that he would have drowned had not a passer-by come to his rescue. To ask whether such incidents really did take place or whether we are to regard them as threads in the colourful rags-to-riches strand of the Verdi tapestry, raises further and more difficult questions. Is literal truth the only kind of truth that matters? With the passage of time, do not the legends inspired by the lives of great men become part of the reality that we recognize and acknowledge?

One of Busseto's prominent citizens was Antonio Barezzi, a prosperous merchant who supplied wine and provisions to shops and taverns in the

12

region. A keen amateur musician who played a variety of wind instruments, including an ophicleide, he was president of the Philharmonic Society of Busseto, who held their meetings in his house. When Carlo Verdi consulted him about his son, Barezzi immediately took a kindly interest in the boy's welfare and was quick to recognize his outstanding musical gifts. He also understood at once the obvious need for proper musical training, and offered a great deal of encouragement and support. The young Verdi took to him at once and responded to his generous nature with an open heart.

On Barezzi's recommendation the *maestro di capella* of the collegiate church of San Bartolemeo, Ferdinando Provesi, who conducted the Philharmonic Society and was director of the municipal school of music, accepted Verdi as his pupil and supervised his musical training for a period of four years. During this time the young musician appeared in public on a number of occasions as a concert pianist. Local music politics blocked an attempt to get him appointed organist at the church of Soragna, where there was a vacancy, but as Provesi's health declined Verdi became his deputy at Busseto cathedral and acted as his assistant in many other ways, taking classes, directing the town band, copying parts, helping during rehearsals and in the preparation of performances. There could hardly have been a better introduction to the art of practical music-making.

While it is true that much of this musical activity went on at a third-rate level compared with what happened in Milan and other great metropolitan centres, it was activity nonetheless. As he later recalled, in his spare time Verdi was encouraged to try his hand at composition:

From my thirteenth to my eighteenth year [the age at which I went to Milan to study counterpoint] I wrote an assortment of pieces, marches for brass band by the hundred; perhaps as many little *sinfonie* that were used in church, in the theatre or at concerts; many serenades, cantatas [arias, duets and very many trios] and various pieces of church music, of which I remember only a *Stabat Mater*.

Verdi's cheerful manner and determination won the admiration of the entire Barezzi household, and now that he was spending so much time with them it was suggested, in May 1831, that he should leave his lodgings and move in with the family. There were two sons and four daughters, the eldest of whom, Margherita, took singing and piano lessons from Verdi. To judge by the striking portrait by Mussini that hangs in the museum at La Scala, she was an attractive young woman with brilliant eyes and an abundance of dark hair setting off a face of fair complexion, full of character and intelligence. She was a few months younger than her tutor, and not surprisingly they soon fell in love.

Barezzi took this new development in his stride – indeed, he may have welcomed it – and determined that further help was needed to advance the career of a potential son-in-law. It was clear that just as Verdi had outstripped the modest training resources available in Le Roncole he was now ready for much more than Busseto could offer. The nearby city of Milan was the only possible place for a more advanced musical education. Carlo Verdi was persuaded to seek a grant from the Monte di Pietá, a local church charity. However, as funds would, at best, be forthcoming from only the second year onwards, Barezzi himself guaranteed tuition fees and other expenses during the first year of study.

At that time it was not possible to travel from one part of Italy to another without formal means of identification. So in June 1832 Giuseppe Verdi obtained the necessary passport, in which he is described as 'tall, with brown hair, black eyebrows and a beard, grey eyes, aquiline nose and small mouth, thin in the face and pale, with pock-marks in his skin'. He then set off for Milan to seek admission to the Conservatorio as a paying pupil. The normal age limit for entry was between nine and fourteen, but the regulations allowed this restriction to be waived for applicants 'of exceptional ability'. Verdi and his supporters had no doubt that he would be admitted on this basis, so their disappointment was the more acute when his application was turned down after a brief examination and an interview with the Director.

The teacher of the pianoforte, Signor Angeleri, declared that Verdi would 'need to change the position of his hand which, at the age of eighteen, would be difficult.' So far as his compositions were concerned he agreed with a colleague that if Verdi 'applies himself attentively and patiently to the rules of counterpoint, he will be able to control the genuine imagination he shows himself to possess and thus turn out creditably as a composer'.

With hindsight it is easy to condemn the Milan authorities for failing to recognize genius in the making, but their difficulties were real enough. The classrooms and the dormitories in the Conservatorio were seriously overcrowded, so the rules about the number of new entrants had to be applied. While the various observations about Verdi himself have as much to say about the narrow, parochial standards of music-making and music training in Busseto as they do about his technical shortcomings, his tense, awkward manner with people he did not know would not have helped his cause, nor would his lack of sophistication and poise. Above all, he was four years late seeking admission. Taking all this into account, the vice-Registrar had little choice in the matter.

One of the examiners to whom Provesi had sent a letter of introduction on behalf of his pupil was Alessandro Rollo, a conductor at La Scala, who advised Verdi to give up the idea of the Conservatorio altogether and to find a teacher in Milan. A director of music at La Scala, Vincenzo Lavigna, was one of those recommended, and it was he who agreed to teach the young man advanced harmony and counterpoint and to give him a thorough grounding in the art of fugal composition.

All this meant extra expense, more than four times the modest grant that had been awarded. Lessons and sheet music had to be paid for as well as board and lodging in the city. Barezzi dug deeper into his pocket and came up with the necessary funds. On Lavigna's advice, he helped Verdi still further in his studies by meeting the cost of his season tickets at the opera, and by giving him a square piano. This, together with the spinet, is also in the museum at La Scala. There followed three years of rigorous training, with the works of Palestrina, Marcello, Bach, Haydn, Mozart and Beethoven held up as worthy of study and examples to follow. Not for the first time in his career Verdi proved to be an extremely receptive and hard-working pupil, but he later confessed that he wrote 'very few ideal compositions.' Apart from two small-scale overtures or *sinfonie* there were 'various pieces, most of them comic, which my master made me do as exercises and which were not even scored.' For the rest it was 'canons and fugues, fugues and canons of all sorts.'

This seems an unusually modest self-assessment, for his tutor's strict academic disciplines were already producing results. When one of the Conservatorio's examiners, Arturo Basily, called on Lavigna to seek his advice about a poor batch of applicants for the vacant post of organist at Monza cathedral, none of whom had been able to write a respectable fugue on a given theme, Verdi was handed the test. While the two professors continued their discussion, the student who had been rejected two years earlier came up with an elegant solution, which he decorated with double counterpoint because, as he dryly observed, the subject itself 'was rather thin'.

Apart from his academic training the young composer was also deriving considerable benefit from his regular visits to La Scala where he was learning, in a less formal way, a great deal about orchestration and the techniques involved in writing music for the stage.

After a busy but uneventful year, news came of the death of his tutor Ferdinando Provesi, followed a month later by that of his sister, Giuseppa Francesca. To his sorrow, he could not afford to make the journey to either funeral. As we have seen, Provesi had played two important roles in the musical life of Busseto, one ecclesiastical, as *maestro di capella* and organist at the church, and the other secular, as municipal music master. Barezzi, as was to be expected, regarded Verdi as a natural successor but Lavigna, on the other hand, insisted that at least another year of formal training was needed before he would be ready to embark upon an independent musical career.

Anxious to please his teacher while remaining loyal to his benefactor, Verdi stayed in Milan to pursue his studies with even greater diligence than before, but sent Barezzi a written application for the post of choirmaster/organist. This was put to one side by the church authorities on the grounds that the vacancy would, in due course, be filled on a competitive basis. However the good priests of Busseto had doubts about Verdi's commitment to the Church, not without reason, and they had already chosen their own safe candidate. His name was Giovanni Ferrari, a local choir-master whose faith was beyond question and who could be confidently relied upon to toe the line. Suddenly, in June 1834, without prior warning or the promised competition, Ferrari was appointed the new *maestro di capella*.

This arbitrary action split the Busseto community down the middle, and the conflict soon became political in nature. Barezzi, at the head of those who supported Verdi, was seen as anti-clerical, not to say dangerously liberal. Those who supported the church were regarded as narrow-minded bigots, right-wing and reactionary. The volatile political atmosphere at that time and the mercurial Italian temperament soon made the crucible of Busseto glow to a dangerous heat.

Members of the Philharmonic Society raided the church and seized all the music they could find to prevent its use. On another occasion the town's brass band drew up outside the church and played as loudly as they could to drown the sound of Ferrari at the organ. Fierce fighting broke out in the streets; graffiti appeared on the walls overnight; threats and counter-threats were flung back and forth; scurrilous lampoons were circulated; dozens of arrests were made and a number of prosecutions followed. Long and alarming reports were sent by the local bishop to the Home Secretary of the Duchy of Parma suggesting that a state of near civil war existed in the town; he urged that the civil and military authorities should be ordered to

'watch attentively, to crush the rebellion at its birth.' While all this mayhem was going on, Verdi was asked by the Milan Philharmonic Society to take over, at very short notice, a rehearsal of Haydn's *The Creation*, after their own conductors had failed to turn up. His grasp of the music and his clear directions so impressed the singers and orchestra that they asked him to conduct the main concert, which was highly successful. A special performance was arranged for a high-ranking audience in the city, and the Austrian governor commanded a further repeat performance to be given at his official residence.

It was a personal triumph of a kind Verdi had not experienced before. Count Romeo Borromeo, the president of the Society, commissioned him to compose a cantata for a forthcoming family wedding; he was asked to conduct a performance of Rossini's *La Cenerentola*, and received an invitation from the Teatro Filodrammatico to write an opera. His enthusiasm for this last project waned when he saw the libretto but, determined not to let the opportunity slip, he persuaded Temistocle Solera, one of his few acquaintances in Milan, to revise the text to follow more closely his own very definite ideas. Other commitments eventually pushed the work to one side and whether any of the music was used later remains a matter for conjecture.

Meanwhile, in July 1835, he had completed his studies and had returned to Busseto, where Barezzi and his supporters continued to do battle on his behalf. By this time Verdi had grown tired of the affair, and his success in the cosmopolitan city of Milan made the prospect of a minor post in a small provincial town much less attractive. As a way out of the dilemma he got Lavigna to support his application for the more lucrative post at Monza cathedral, which was still vacant. But when some of the Busseto Philharmonic Society members heard about this they were furious and reminded Verdi of his obligations to the town. Some went so far as to suggest that if he tried to leave, he would be prevented from doing so by force. In the face of such hostility and to save Barezzi's position he dropped the Monza idea, as he explained to Lavigna:

If my benefactor Barezzi would not have had to suffer on my account the almost general hostility of the district, I should have left at once; neither their reproaches about benefits not their threats would have been able to affect me. Even if I did receive from the Monte di pietá a slender pension towards my support in Milan, this benefit ought not to purchase my degradation and slavery, or I should be obliged to consider the said benefit no longer a generous act, but a mean one.

Three months later, in an attempt bring the bitter controversy in Busseto to an end, the church put forward a compromise plan. Duties previously undertaken by Provesi would be divided: Ferrari would remain church organist, but the post of *maestro di musica* would now be filled by competition. If he chose to do so, Verdi would be allowed to apply. Why so obvious a solution had taken so long to emerge is unknown, but Barezzi and his supporters saw it as a victory. They believed that the result of any competition was beyond any doubt: this time they were right. Verdi was examined at Parma by the venerable Giuseppe Alinovi, who told him 'he had enough knowledge to be *maestro* in Paris or London.' Within weeks his contract of employment came through. With his years of study now behind him and the prospect of secure, if modest, income ahead, Verdi felt that he could now ask Barezzi for his daughter's hand.

After a brief engagement they were married on 4 May 1836. They had two children, both of whom died in infancy. Virginia Maria Luigia was born in March 1837 and died in August 1838. Her brother, Icilio Romano Carlo Antonio, was then only a few weeks old: he, in turn, died at the age of fifteen months in October 1839. The death of infants always has a special poignancy but these dates are significant for other reasons, which will become apparent later.

Verdi's contract was for nine years, but after three it could be terminated by either side at six months' notice. He had to live in Busseto ten months of the year, to give vocal and instrumental lessons in the municipal school and to conduct Philharmonic Society concerts. He kept to his side of the bargain conscientiously, but still found irksome the reminders that he was under an obligation to the community for the support he had been given. Such narrow-mindedness was offensive to him, and strengthened his resolve to make his mark outside Busseto. After his successes in Milan he knew that it was to the wider world he belonged.

So, in addition to the many sacred and secular compositions he wrote for local performance, he continued to work on larger-scale projects such as the opera which had been suggested by his friend Massini, of the Teatro Filodrammatico. 'Such as' is a necessary evasion at this point since much confusion surrounds the gestation of Verdi's first published opera, a confusion made worse by his own inaccurate recollections in later life. According to some biographers he started *Oberto* in 1836; others say it is an adaptation of a previous work, *Rocester*. It has also been suggested that an even earlier attempt, *Lord Hamilton*, now completely lost, may have been the original upon which *Oberto* is based. Julian Budden, in his classic three-volume work *The Operas of Verdi* has yet another possible explanation. The composer may have taken with him:

a rough and ready operatic structure in the conventional mould, to be expanded, shortened or generally modified, in accordance with the singers available for the first performance, and based on a story which could adapt itself, chameleon-like, to medieval Italy no less than to Restoration England.

Wherever the truth lies, Verdi now had enough confidence in his powers to cancel the contract of employment by mutual consent. In February 1839 he left Busseto and took his wife and their surviving son to the great city of Milan, where he rented a modest flat near the basilica of Sant'Ambrogio to be within easy walking distance of La Scala.

He had waited in the wings long enough: the time had come for Giuseppe Verdi to make his entrance on to the world's operatic stage.

Chapter 2

Reality Invented

When the time came for Verdi's first opera to go into rehearsal Massini was no longer director of the Teatro Filodrammatico and was therefore unable to help directly. However, he did promise to 'try every means' to have the work performed at La Scala 'on the occasion of the benefit concert for the Pio Istituto . . . '. Verdi goes on:

> Eventually everything was arranged for the spring of 1839, in which case I would have had four truly outstanding singers: Strepponi, the tenor Moriani, the baritone Giorgio Ronconi and the bass Marini. But no sooner were the parts distributed and the piano rehearsals begun than Marini became seriously ill . . .

The production had to be abandoned, and the composer was plunged into despair. He even considered returning to Busseto. His disappointment was shared by the young soprano Giuseppina Strepponi, who had hoped that her debut at La Scala would set the seal on a highly successful career.

At the age of twenty-four Strepponi was at the height of her beauty and of her musical powers. With her large, expressive eyes, her dark hair drawn tightly back to reveal a perfectly-formed oval face, her long white neck and gently-sloping shoulders, she was what we would now recognize as the archetypal Romantic heroine. But to her contemporaries she was an exciting new presence on the operatic stage, sweeping away the old rhetorical conventions with a simplicity of style in her singing and in her acting. One critic described her voice as 'flexible and wide-ranging, her figure nimble and her dramatic talent notable.' It is not difficult to imagine her reaching out to her audiences and holding them in her thrall, like Maria Callas of a much later generation. She was in every respect the *prima donna assoluta* of her time.

Strepponi had heard about Verdi from her fellow performers, and there is some evidence to suggest that she had actually seen a piano reduction of the score of *Rocester* and had been impressed by it. But it was not until work started on *Oberto* that his music really caught her attention, as did its handsome young composer when she first saw him in rehearsal.

Her reputation as a singer was matched only by her notoriety. It was common gossip in Milan that she had had an illegitimate child by the impresario Bartolomeo Merelli, who was manager of La Scala and of the Kärntnertortheater in Vienna. Whether Strepponi had succeeded in persuading Merelli that Verdi's opera was worth staging, or whether he

Count Oberto's daughter, Leonora, has been seduced by Riccardo, who abandons her for his bride-to-be, Cuniza. Enraged by such treachery and the dishonour done to his family the elderly Count challenges Riccardo who, like Don Giovanni, has no wish to fight an old man. The women try to prevent bloodshed, but the opponents make for a wood where Oberto is killed in the duel. Filled with remorse, Riccardo goes into voluntary exile after leaving all his property to his first love, Leonora.

had overheard her enthusing about the music is not altogether clear.

But as the disappointed composer made arrangements to return to Busseto he was asked to call on Merelli, who told him that if he made certain revisions to *Oberto, Conte di San Bonifacio* he would be offered a contract, and would receive half of the net profit. Furthermore, he would not be asked to guarantee a share of the production costs, the usual practice with works of new and untried composers. Merelli knew very well that Verdi was already in debt and unable to meet such a condition. Strepponi may have made it her business to tell him.

Preparations for the opera were well under way when the second tragedy struck the young family. Less than a month before the premiere of *Oberto* the surviving child, Icilio, contracted pneumonia and died on 22 October 1839. 'The poor little boy, languishing, died in the arms of his totally desperate mother,' was how the composer described the loss many years later. When the opening night came, Margherita could not bear to dress up for the theatre and pretend to enjoy herself. So between the two acts of the opera, Verdi ran back to the flat, took his wife into his arms, and assured her that all was going well.

The plot of *Oberto* is simple enough, but already reveals Verdi's taste for larger-than-life characters, melodramatic situations and the deep understanding of father-daughter relationships so often found in his later operas. 'For a first opera *Oberto* is an interesting achievement', writes Julian Budden, 'but let us not exaggerate . . . had Verdi died after writing it, he would not be remembered today.' Substantial changes were made to the score and new material added for revivals in Turin, Genoa, Naples and Milan during the 1840s.

A rare opportunity for a modern audience to judge the work was given in Leeds in 1994. Music critic Rodney Milnes was present on that occasion and described the music as 'pretty rough and ready; some of it is out of early 19th century stock, but it is good stock; occasionally very fine, with many a pre-echo of what was to come.'

Verdi himself was harsher in his judgement, as he was of many of his early works, and did his best to prevent a revival at La Scala in 1889 to mark the fiftieth anniversary of the premiere. This was a gala occasion to be attended by the King of Italy, his prime minister and many of the country's leading citizens. Verdi expressed his feelings in a letter to his distinguished librettist, Arrigo Boito:

Can you believe that today's public, with tastes so different from those of fifty years ago, ever would have the patience to sit through

OBERTO

CONTE DI S. BONIFACIO

DRAMMA IN DUE ATTI

DA RAPPRESENTARSI

NELL' I. R. TEATRO ALLA SCALA

L' AUTUNNO 1839.

Milano

PER GASPARE TRUFFI

M.DCCC.XXXIX

The title page of the libretto of *Oberto*, printed in 1839.

two long acts of *Oberto*! Either they would be bored to death in polite silence (always a humiliating affair), or they would demonstrate their disapproval!

However, the first-night audience of 1839, reared on a conventional diet of Bellini, Rossini, Mercadante, Ricci and Donizetti, gave a warm welcome to the new composer and to his opera, which received fourteen further performances. This was a reasonable run at that time, especially for a maiden work, and seemed to confirm Merelli's judgement and skill in backing a winner. He offered Verdi a contract for three more operas over a two-year term, for production either at La Scala or at the Kärntnertortheater in Vienna. Verdi gives his own account of this transaction:

. . . he was to pay me 4,000 Austrian lire for each opera, sharing with me the proceeds from the sale of the scores. I accepted the contract at once; and a little while later Merelli left for Vienna, having told the poet Rossi to send me a libretto. However, I wasn't very happy about it and I hadn't even started setting it to music by the time Merelli got back to Milan in the early months of 1840, and said that he really must have a comedy for the autumn season . . .

Once again the composer rejected many of the libretti put in front of him, but because 'the matter was of some urgency' he set misgivings aside and chose a text, 'which seemed to me the least bad'. This was one written by Felice Romani nearly thirty years earlier: its original title *Il finto Stanislao* was changed to *Un giorno di regno* (King for a Day).

No sooner had Verdi started work on this new project than he suffered a severe attack of angina, from which he made only a slow and uncertain recovery. While doing so he realized that he had been unable to set aside enough money to pay the rent on his flat [fifty crowns], due in three days time. His young wife sensed his anxiety: she took from her jewellery box the few valuable pieces she had and, without telling her husband, used them as security on a loan. 'I was deeply touched by this tender affection,' he wrote, 'and promised myself to buy everything back again in a very short time . . . thanks to my agreement with Merelli.'

Verdi was not to have known that there remained all too little time for him to make good his promise, for within a few weeks Margherita fell ill and, despite desperate efforts by her doctors to save her life, died on 18 June 1840. The following entry appears in the diary of Antonio Barezzi:

In Milan at midday on the feast of Corpus Christi my beloved daughter Margherita died in my arms of some terrible disease perhaps unknown to medical science; she was in the flower of her youth and at the height of her good fortune, for she had become the lifelong companion of that excellent young man Giuseppe Verdi, *maestro di musica*.

The terrible disease was almost certainly encephalitis, which could not be diagnosed at that time and for which no treatment existed, then as now. Overcome with grief, 'having seen a third coffin carried out the house', Verdi returned with his father-in-law to Busseto and pleaded with Merelli to release him entirely from his contract.

But the impresario refused and insisted on the opera being ready on time. Whether he did this to protect his own interests is difficult to judge, but from what we know of the man it would have been entirely in character for him to have realised that the only way to help Verdi was to have him work through his grief. And so, two months later, the young widower returned to Milan 'in the midst of terrible sorrow to compose and to see through to its production a comic opera.'

The complicated and only partly-resolved plot of *Un giorno di regno* relies on such well-worn comic opera conventions as crossed lovers, mistaken identities and double weddings, and is based on an improbable story about King Stanislaus Leszczynski of Poland. The reaction of the audience was extremely unfavourable. According to one local critic 'the singers, who hardly bothered to sing, got confused amidst a storm of catcalls.' Merelli promptly withdrew the piece after the first night and filled the gaps in his schedule with works from La Scala's standard repertoire.

It was the first time Verdi had been obliged to face a hostile press, and the experience soured his attitude towards journalists and critics. But there was at least one perceptive and sympathetic comment that came from the music critic of *Figaro*, who observed that he

> . . . was forced to clothe his latest work with gay music just at the time when a cruel and unexpected catastrophe had struck him in the innermost part of his being, and it will be easily understood how in his second venture he fell short of the expectations aroused by his first.

Verdi later admitted that his music was partly to blame, adding that the performance also played a substantial part in the fiasco. Overwhelmed by grief and embittered by the failure he could find 'no consolation' in his art and 'decided never to compose again.'

He asked for his contract to be returned, but Merelli treated him like 'a naughty child' and said very firmly that he should not allow himself to be discouraged by one setback. But when Verdi insisted, the document was produced and handed back to him. 'I can't make you compose by force,' said Merelli, 'but my confidence in you remains. Who knows? One day you may well decide to take up your pen again. In which case, you have only to give me two months' notice before the season starts and I promise to put on whatever you send me.'

For the next three months Verdi virtually went to ground. He took a small flat in an out-of-the-way part of Milan in which he nursed his wounds and spent much of his time reading 'bad romances and yellow-covered novels'. If we are to believe his own account, he seldom went out and never touched his piano. But on a snowy January evening in 1841, on a rare venture out-of-doors, he happened to bump into Merelli, who grabbed his arm and walked him back to La Scala, chatting all the way.

The impresario told Verdi that he was in great trouble: he had asked Otto Nicolai to write a new opera but the German composer was not at all satisfied with the libretto. 'Can you imagine,' said Merelli, 'a libretto by Solera, superb! . . . magnificent! . . . extraordinary! . . . but this obstinate Nicolai will not hear of it and declares that it's impossible . . . I would give anything to find another immediately.'

Verdi would have none of this, and blandly suggested a way out of the difficulty. 'Didn't you have *Il Proscritto* written for me?' he asked. 'I haven't composed a single note, and I put it entirely at your disposal.' When they reached his office Merelli scooped up Solera's manuscript from his desk, saying 'So fine a subject – and to refuse it! You take it: you read it!', and despite Verdi's protests the 'large paper book' was thrust into his hands. He rolled it up, shoved it into his pocket, took his leave and trudged back through the snow to his lodgings.

As I walked, I felt myself seized with a kind of undefinable uneasiness; a profound sadness, a genuine anguish took possession of my heart. I went into my room, and with an impatient gesture I threw the manuscript on the table, and remained standing before it. In falling on the table it had opened by itself; without knowing how, my eyes fixed on a page which was before me and on this verse: '*Va, pensiero, sull' ali dorate* ['Fly, thoughts, on wings of gold'] I ran through the verses that followed and was much moved, all the more because they were almost a paraphrase from the Bible, the reading of which had always delighted me.

I read one passage and then another. Then resolute in my determination to write no more, I forced myself to close the libretto and retired to bed. But to no avail – I couldn't get Nabucco out of my mind. Unable to sleep, I got up and read the text not once, but two or three times, so that by morning I knew Solera's libretto by heart.

That is Verdi's account of what happened.

Once again, we would do well to bear in mind that his sense of drama was more dependable than his memory. Need it be said that for the script to fall open to reveal the line that was to make him famous throughout Italy and the world beyond is another bit of melodrama, another example of invented reality? Did any of this really take place? Writing ten years earlier than Verdi's own reminiscences, Michele Lessona tells us that on returning to his lodgings the composer flung the libretto into a corner of his room without giving it a single glance, and that it stayed there undisturbed for five months. This simpler, less romantic version of events was endorsed by the great man himself: 'that is my story for you,' he wrote to his friend Count Opprandino Arrivabene, 'as true as true can be'.

How serious were his intentions to give up writing music after the disastrous failure of *Un giorno di regno*? How did he expect make ends meet in Milan, since the revenue from his two operas could not have kept him in funds for very long?

These are among the questions posed by Julian Budden in his great study of the operas. He points out that Verdi seems to have written 'two substantial new numbers for the revival of *Oberto* at La Scala that same winter; and he supervised and rehearsed a new production at Genoa in January 1841, again adding fresh music.' Hardly the actions of someone who had kept his piano lid closed and had shut himself away from all work and social contact. 'It would seem' suggests Budden, with a nice touch of irony, 'that youthful resilience triumphed earlier than he remembered or wanted us to believe.'

There are other discrepancies more baffling than these. In later life he described how his young wife and their two children died within the space of three months while he worked on his ill-fated comic opera. We know that this is not correct. 'Such a mistake surely shows how these bereavements became etched on his memory as a single and terrible tragedy,' suggests one his biographers, Peter Southwell-Sander.

Is this so, or was there some instinct at work that prompted Verdi always to heighten the drama of already dramatic situations, as if he were in some way editing and improving the libretto of an opera based on his own remarkable life-story? Or as he grew older did he decide to throw dust into the eyes of would-be biographers, a breed of men and women he liked little more than critics and journalists?

'In the end it all depends on a libretto, a libretto, a libretto and the opera is made!' he wrote in 1865. And in a letter to his friend the Countess Maffei he declared, 'It may be a good thing to copy reality; but to invent it is much, much better!'

Verdi's falsification – it is not too strong a word – of details that might otherwise have revealed the exact nature of his relationship with Giuseppina Strepponi at that time, is another example of invention of reality. Only on this delicate matter he was at pains to reduce the element of drama, not to enhance it. He was supported in his efforts by the *prima donna* herself, as Gaia Servadio describes:

> . . . [they] went to great lengths to construct fictitious versions of their lives, omitting whatever struck them as inappropriate – what-

ever might have caused scandal in the prevailing nineteenth century morality. Their individual accounts are often contradictory: at times this might be due simply to the erratic memory of old age, confusing dates and events, but more often it was the result of a conscious intention to change the truth. Had he been unfaithful during the build-up to *Oberto*, Giuseppe Verdi would have denied it later: how could he ever have confessed an adventure with a celebrated singer, when he was living just a stone's throw away with a young and grief-stricken wife?

Among all the uncertainties and conjectures one fact stands out: by the autumn of 1841 Verdi had completed the score of *Nabucco*. Reminding Merelli of his promise, he confidently suggested that the new opera should be staged during the 1842 carnival season. Merelli was ready to honour his word, but explained that already he had accepted three new works for

A portrait by an unknown artist of Giuseppina Strepponi, who was the leading soprano of her day. She earned huge fees, and through her various liaisons wielded great power behind the scenes of Italian opera.

the coming season and could not possibly risk a fourth. Verdi was furious, and sent Merelli an intemperate letter of which he was later much ashamed. 'Is this the way to treat an old friend? asked the aggrieved impresario. Nevertheless he conceded Verdi's point and agreed to produce *Nabucco*, at the same time making it clear that existing props and scenery, prepared for a ballet on the same theme, would have to be used in order to reduce costs.

The story of *Nabucco* goes back to the Apocrypha and the account of the Assyrian invasion of Judaea early in the sixth century B.C. under their powerful leader King Nebuchadnezzar. The libretto by Temistocle Solera, who earlier had worked with Verdi on *Oberto*, acknowledges also a much more contemporary source, *Nabucodonosor*, a play by Anicet-Bourgeois and Francis Cornus first performed in Paris in 1836 and read throughout Italy in translation.

The first performance of *Nabucco* took place at La Scala on 9 March 1842, after only twelve days of rehearsal. At the end of Act 1 there was such an uproar in the house that Verdi, who in accordance with custom was seated among the orchestra, thought for one moment that some members of the audience were after him. And in a sense they were, but to show their enthusiasm, not their disapproval. After *Va, pensiero* they refused to allow the performance to continue without an encore. The people of Milan, increasingly resentful of Austrian domination, could hardly fail to identify themselves with the Jews and their patriotic chorus. In theory, encores were banned by the police because they were all too likely to turn into hostile demonstrations against Austrian officials and their wives, seated in the more expensive boxes. In practice, conductors usually gave way, pleading that to resist popular demand might entail even greater risk. This happened on the opening night, but because the plot was taken from the Bible *Nabucco* was a difficult opera for the authorities to censor. The political implications were not lost on Verdi's public and when the curtain fell on Act 4, audience and orchestra rose together in a standing ovation, cheering and applauding the composer and singers for minutes on end.

Curiously, the critics of the day did not single out for special mention the *Va, pensiero* chorus despite its obvious appeal, musically and politically, to the Milanese audience. Possibly they failed to recognize a popular hit when they heard it, or perhaps they were unwilling to run the risk of reprisals from the censors. Others have suggested that Verdi was not yet a person of sufficient stature to be exploited by those with a political axe to grind, and that 'his reputation as a "patriotic influence" in 19th century Italy was a creation of later generations.'

Nevertheless, the remaining seven performances during that 1842 spring season each drew a similarly enthusiastic response, which prompted Merelli to revive the piece no fewer than 57 times during the following autumn – a record for La Scala that stands to this day. The composer's fame spread rapidly. 'All over Italy,' according to the American writer George Martin, 'as the opera passed from town to town, Italian patriots heard in that chorus their own emotions after failing so often to end their Austrian captivity.' Productions soon followed elsewhere across Europe and throughout the rest of the world: in less than a decade *Nabucco* was heard and seen in cities as far afield as Buenos Aires, Havana,

Constantinople, Budapest, St Petersburg, Copenhagen and New York. It reached London in 1846, although before the work could be staged the story had to be rewritten on account of its Biblical content, and the title changed to *Nino, Re d'Assyria*.

After *Nabucco* Giuseppe Verdi could take his place among the front rank of Italian opera composers. This was the work, as he later recalled, that marked the true start of his artistic career. Never again did he have to seek commissions; they came to him, and in such numbers that he was almost overwhelmed.

Leaders of fashionable society in Milan joined the Countess Maffei in opening the doors of their *salons* to the young composer, who 'suddenly found himself beset by a crowd of friends who needed to tell him how they had always loved him,' as Lessona crisply observed. Verdi himself came to believe that *Nabucco* was 'born under a lucky star'. 'The first scene in the temple, for instance, produced such an effect that the audience applauded for ten minutes,' he notes with satisfaction, listing those aspects of the

Poster for the autumn season at La Scala in 1842.

Clara Maffei (1814-86).

production that might have gone disastrously wrong but which, in the event, went triumphantly right. However, true to character, he concludes that it does not always do to trust in lucky stars. 'Experience has taught me the truth of the proverb *To trust is good, but not to trust is better.*'

The years of apprenticeship were at an end, but the long years in the *galera* – to use his own expression – were about to begin. Variously translated as 'prison' or 'galley', it is a word full of resonances, some of which are associated with slave ships, and, by association, with slavery. As a very old man looking back on his crucial years that is how Verdi saw himself, as a slave to his genius and to the most demanding of his many mistresses, opera.

Chapter 3

Mercenaries of the Theatre

The craze for opera in Italy – and it was nothing less than a craze – was almost at its peak by the time Verdi arrived on the scene. Every major city in the country, and virtually every small town, boasted at least one opera house. Many of them were built to a conventional horseshoe plan which gave the audience a clear view of the stage, of the performers and, no less important, of each other. Competition was intense, each community determined that its own opera house should be more splendid than those of its neighbours. To satisfy such harmless municipal pride, florid and elaborate decorations in abundance were added to designs already conceived in flamboyant rococo style.

Throughout Europe theatres and opera houses followed the Italian pattern. This scene in a box at the Paris Opéra in 1843 is by John Henry Robinson.

As a way of funding original building costs, boxes were either sold outright or let out on a long-term lease like any other piece of real estate.

In many cases the contract included the use of a room on the other side of a main corridor, facing the box, where food and drink could be prepared and served to the owners and their guests by a flurry of servants clad in livery.

The arrangement of boxes in tiers, up to as many as six in number, not only made the best possible use of space but also reflected the social order of the time. The largest and most expensive boxes were usually to be found on the second tier, arranged either side of a central box reserved for the local prince and his family. The upper tiers presented a reverse image of the pecking order: the lower your standing, the higher your place in the opera house. The only exceptions were to be found among the middle-class members of the audience who usually sat in the stalls, where seats with arm-rests were charged extra.

Galleries, where they existed at all, were occupied by the lower orders. But even the cheapest ticket represented at least a day's wages for a peasant or a labourer, with the result that those on the bottom rung of the social ladder – even those with a taste for formal music – were rarely to be seen in an opera house. The Italian proverb makes the point: 'bed is the poor man's opera.'

Behind the ornate facades and the gilded cherubs, the angels with trumpets, the swirling drapes, the grand cartouches and the cornucopia laden with fruit, there was an almost total lack of facilities modern audiences take for granted. For many opera houses and theatres were built at a time when Italians paid much less regard to public hygiene than did their Roman ancestors, as foreign visitors discovered to their cost. One of them, Mrs Gladstone, wife of the future British prime minister, during a visit to Naples, was so overcome by the stench in one of the city's smaller opera houses, the inappropriately named *Teatro Nuovo*, that she had to leave well before the end of the performance.

However, it is fortunate that many of the traditional opera houses in Italy have survived to the present day, having been suitably modernised without great loss to the original fabric or decor. With their spacious foyers, numerous anterooms, wide stairways and corridors it is easy to understand how these magnificent buildings were centres for community life as a whole, and not only places where opera, ballet and masked balls were staged at certain times of the year.

Generally speaking, these seasons were during the pre-Lenten carnival period, and during the spring and autumn at times carefully chosen to avoid the hottest weather, especially in southern Italy. Serious opera was not the only fare on offer. More popular tastes were catered for by the major houses during their off-seasons, and by smaller, cheaper theatres throughout the year, where there was a choice of entertainment ranging from sentimental, middle-brow operas and plays, through *opera buffa*, comedies and farce to puppet shows and circus acts complete with performing animals.

For the more educated, wealthier classes and those nobly-born (it is necessary to make the distinction), the principal opera house was the place in which to be seen, not once or twice a season, but night after night. Only in this way could ambitions be advanced and established positions maintained. Visits to the opera were social and family events as well as musical occasions to be enjoyed, with the result that there was a continuous buzz of chatter from the audience. Only when a particularly demanding aria or an intricate ensemble came along was much attention paid to the music or to what was happening on the stage.

However, when singers actually succeeded in gaining the audience's ear they were followed knowledgeably and with care. An aria well performed was often rewarded by murmurs of encouragement and approval, followed by cries of *Bravo!* at its conclusion. On the other hand poor singers were frequently assailed by a storm of jeers and catcalls, and if they really upset the audience they would be hissed off the stage.

Reactions of this kind were not always as genuine or as spontaneous as they appeared, for most of the leading opera houses had a resident *claque* or faction – a group of hirelings paid to cheer on impresarios and singers or to shout down their rivals. In a tradition that dates back to classical times these mercenaries of the theatre wielded considerable influence, and continue to do so to this day. This is especially the case in France and in Italy where, as Harold Rosenthal has said, 'the drama of opera-going extends well beyond the footlights'. Tariffs were issued showing the payments expected for such services as applause on entry, shouts of *Bene!*, *Bravo!* or other signs of approval, demands for encores and 'expressions of wild enthusiasm.'

A convention which might seem invidious, not to say corrupt, to those accustomed to less partisan ways of listening to opera, is not without its defenders. *Claqueurs* themselves claim that they help to maintain standards by offering encouragement to those with genuine talent; that they are no more unscrupulous than advertising or public relations men engaged in promoting up-and-coming singers, and that frequently they act with greater integrity and musical understanding than established critics. In Parma, for example, the local *claque* once returned a fee paid by a visiting tenor because his performance was so dreadful, and went back to the theatre the following evening to hiss him loudly, free of charge. In more recent times, rival *claques* came to blows when Maria Callas appeared in Milan: two of the rioters were arrested during the performance and were later sent to prison.

Such active participation from the auditorium disconcerted, and still disconcerts, visitors from abroad. Berlioz complained that Italian audiences 'consume their operas like a plate of macaroni.' But many Italian opera-goers, even today, would find it impossible to listen for a whole evening sitting in respectful silence, responding only to the more obvious cues for applause. Indeed, they would probably regard such behaviour as highly unnatural, indicating a lack of musical appreciation, knowledge and taste. To the Italians opera has always been a great deal more than a passive spectator sport.

Visitors from abroad would also have been struck by the number of resplendent uniforms to be seen in a typical Italian audience at that time. Some were military; off-duty junior officers in the front stalls, for example, determined to get the best possible view of the young ladies of the chorus or of the *corps de ballet*. Other uniforms belonged to police officers of various levels of seniority, who kept guard in many parts of the building as well as in the auditorium itself. They came under the command of a senior government official with his own box in the theatre, who had wide powers to take whatever action he considered necessary to maintain public order.

Tito Ricordi (1811-88), son of Giovanni Ricordi, who founded the great Milan music publishing house. He took over the firm on his father's death, and became a close friend of the composer.

There were rules against noisy applause, encores and curtain calls before the end of an act, but they were not always strictly enforced. Opera texts (*libretti*) were scrutinized to ensure they contained no subversive matter likely to upset Italy's Austrian rulers, but the censors were just as concerned not to allow anything on the stage that might give offence to the Church or to the authorities generally. Their job was to preserve the fabric of society and to prevent unseemly disturbances from taking place. Certainly before the revolutions of 1848 political censorship was exercised erratically and could not fairly be described as repressive.

This was especially true of Milan, where the regime was regarded as almost liberal. The city's Austrian censors raised no objection to the *Va, pensiero* chorus in *Nabucco*, just as Verdi himself raised no objection when his publisher, Giovanni Ricordi, inscribed on the title page of the vocal part of the opera a dedication to 'Her Royal Highness the Most Serene Archduchess Adelaide of Austria'. Much the same thing happened when Verdi's next opera, *I Lombardi*, was staged. At one point the Lombards cry out *La Santa Terra oggi nostra sarà* ('Today the Holy Land

The interior of La Scala, Milan, where Verdi's early operas were first performed.

will be ours'). That chorus was also greeted with enthusiasm by the Milanese audience, and the opera from which it came was dedicated to another pillar of the Establishment, the Duchess Marie Louise of Parma.

Italian singers and instrumentalists were renowned all over Europe and in the Americas but, then as now, competition was fierce, opportunities were few, and only musicians of exceptional ability and good fortune were able to make a real success of their careers. For the most part, life for a professional was harsh and dispiriting. Singers counted themselves lucky if they found a place in a local choir or opera chorus, while instrumental players and budding young conductors vied jealously with each other whenever a permanent post became vacant in one of the municipal or theatre pit orchestras. By the mid-19th century the patronage of the Church, never one of the more generous employers, was in decline and wealthy patrons had become fewer in number. As a result, most musicians were poorly paid and had to augment their meagre incomes by teaching, taking in pupils, or by undertaking such humble tasks as the copying of parts.

Shortage of money was not the only difficulty to be overcome in the pursuit of a professional musical career, for there remained a strong prejudice against those who earned their living by appearing in public on the stage. On the whole this prejudice bore down more heavily on women, who were more vulnerable to gossip and whose morals were always subject to greater scrutiny, than upon men, from whom less exacting standards of conduct were demanded or expected. The majority of performers came from fairly modest backgrounds, and rigorous musical training allowed very little time for cultivating the more elegant social graces or widening educational backgrounds. Whether attitudes have changed much during the past 150 years or so seems rather doubtful. In an interview he gave in 1989 the well-known British conductor, Sir Simon Rattle, said that although he greatly admired Italian opera, he had no wish to conduct it. 'One does actually want to hear it sung by the kind of people one wouldn't want to have dinner with!'

The early years of nineteenth century opera in Italy were over-shadowed by Gioacchino Rossini (1792-1868), whose comic operas have remained firm favourites. His more serious works, such as *Ermione*, are now returning to the repertoire.

Personal rivalries were often intense, but the hardships and the prejudices endured by those in the theatrical and musical professions, which were closely linked at that time, produced a strong sense of fellowship and camaraderie. In their dealings with those in authority, or with people who might in some way further their careers, musicians and actors could be ingratiating to an extent that most modern patrons would find distasteful. This is partly accounted for by the manners and customs of the times, of course, but also by the fundamental insecurity most of them felt. Among themselves they were direct, robust and full of sardonic humour, like most communities who face adversity in common. As John Rosselli, expert on the social history of opera, has observed: ' . . . for much of the nineteenth century the musical profession remained largely insulated from the rest of society, a traditional craft, most of whose members liked to work, eat, talk, joke, quarrel and make love with each other far more than with anybody else.'

Working conditions for singers and players in theatres and opera houses were hard. Most companies were required to present two new operas each season which meant, in practice, that the second opera had to be rehearsed

Vincenzo Bellini (1801-35) was, like Rossini, one of the leading opera composers in the bel canto tradition. Despite the great success of *Norma*, *La Sonnambula*, *I Puritani* and other works, it was a tradition in decline by the time Verdi came onto the scene in the 1840s.

while the first was being presented to the public. It has been estimated that on average singers had no more than 15 days to master a principal role. If an opera failed and the run had to be abandoned preparation times for a replacement work could be even shorter. Moreover, outside the really top-rank houses the same cast was expected to appear four or five times a week, which placed the severest strain on soloists, many of whom over-taxed their voices and were obliged to give up their singing careers at an early age.

Giuseppina Strepponi was one of many singers who suffered in this way. While pregnant, she performed the leading role in Bellini's *Norma* no fewer than six times in one week: the strain proved too great and she suffered a miscarriage. She was only 26 years old when she had to abandon the important role of Abigaille in *Nabucco*. Not all authorities are agreed, but it seems likely that Verdi had Strepponi in his mind's ear, at the height of her powers, when he created the part for her. But when it came to actual performance, not even he could support her determination to carry on. Donizetti, among others, was highly critical and after her first few appearances she was obliged to hand over to Teresa di Giuli Borsi, a singer she had once vividly described as 'a bird of prey scavenging among corpses.'

Verdi could no longer rely on Strepponi's outstanding qualities as a singer, but he had the wit to realise that her knowledge and experience of the operatic world, and her shrewd business sense, could be of great value to him. After the triumph of *Nabucco*, Merelli had decided to commission Verdi to compose one of the new works required for the following season, the so-called *opera di obbligo*. It was a great honour to be chosen, especially for a composer whose career was not yet fully established. And in drawing up the contract the impresario had taken care to leave blank the amount to be paid. In other words, he invited Verdi to name his price.

The composer was completely out of his depth. He was not used to ploys of this kind, so he sought Giuseppina's advice. She told him that he should ask not less than eight thousand Austrian *lire*, the huge sum paid eleven years earlier to Vincenzo Bellini for *Norma*. It was advice of breath-taking audacity, for this record figure had gone to a highly-respected composer at the peak of his career and reputation, and not to an up-and-coming young contender with one overnight success to his credit. But Strepponi's assessment of the situation was absolutely right: Merelli, who was making a great deal of money from *Nabucco*, signed the contract without question, much to Verdi's delight and astonishment. Verdi never forgot this crucial episode so early in his career: neither did he forget the one who had given him such clear-headed counsel.

There is a sad irony in that as Strepponi's star in the fashionable salons of Milan waned, so Verdi's shone with increasing brilliance. Despite his gauche manner, society hostesses were at pains to get his name on their guest lists. To his surprise – and embarrassment – he came to be regarded as a spokesman for the revolution against Austrian rule. He was pointed out in the streets of Milan; stews and sauces were named after him: young men, and some not so young, copied the way he dressed, and even the cut of his beard and his hair-style.

Overnight he had become the man of the hour.

Among the many doors now open to him were those of the brilliant salon of the poet Cavaliere Andrea Maffei and his wife, the Contessa Clara Maffei, who was an ardent supporter of the *Risorgimento*, the movement dedicated to the political unification and independence of Italy. Its leader, Giuseppe Mazzini, described by George Martin as 'a tall, thin, passionate young man from Genoa who could write with the force of an Old Testament prophet', was among the many frequent visitors to the Maffei household. Other patriots included Tommaso Grossi, on whose poem Solera was to base the libretto for Verdi's next opera, *I Lombardi*, and Carlo Tenca, who wrote articles for the music journals and had an eye firmly fixed on the Contessa herself.

Count Opprandino Arrivabene was another critic who regularly visited the Casa Maffei, together with Arrigo Boito, a composer who was destined to become the most famous of all Verdi's librettists. Verdi himself responded warmly to the intellectual and cultural stimulus of the salon with its added, slightly dangerous, element of patriotic and republican fervour, and much enjoyed the company of the influential figures he met there, many of whom became close personal friends.

Andrea Maffei, sixteen years older than his wife, was less interested in

politics but surrounded himself with the leading literary figures of the day. He achieved great notoriety for his gambling and wild *affaires*, which proved too much even for Milanese society, and in 1846 the couple separated under a cloud of scandal. The formal deed of separation was witnessed by Verdi, who remained on good terms with them both. He had set three of Maffei's poems to music in 1845, and later asked the poet to help him with the text of *Macbeth*, and to provide a full libretto for *I masnadieri*, first produced in 1847 at Her Majesty's Theatre in London. All these events the future held in store: of more immediate concern to Verdi at this time was the choice of subject for his next opera.

Chapter 4

A Strong Smell
of Garlic Sausages

Merelli and Verdi knew when they were on to a good thing. As a follow-up to *Nabucco* they chose a topic striking the same resonant chords of freedom and patriotism to which their audiences had already responded with such enthusiasm. Tommaso Grossi's *I Lombardi alla prima Crociata* (The Lombards at the First Crusade), an epic poem written in 1826, contained the right ingredients – exiles in a hostile land united against a common foe, fervent calls for freedom and liberty with thinly-veiled references to independence and national pride – these were all Solera needed for his libretto.

This time their plans did not go unnoticed. The Archbishop of Milan took the first step by drawing attention to a proposed scene depicting a baptism, to which he took grave exception. He also expressed displeasure that some of the later action was set near the Holy City of Jerusalem.

Impresario, composer and librettist were summoned to a meeting with Torresani, the chief of police and a known music-lover. Verdi refused to attend, letting it be known that the opera would be staged uncut and uncensored, or not at all. With only Solera to support him Merelli used his diplomatic skills to persuade Torresani not to take the matter further. As a gesture to the Archbishop, however, it was agreed that Giselda's prayer to the Virgin Mary in the second scene of Act I should be altered to read *Salve Maria* instead of *Ave Maria*.

The first performance of *I Lombardi* came up to the expectations of Merelli and his collaborators, and more than justified the fears harboured

---

I LOMBARDI ALLA PRIMA CROCIATA
Teatro alla Scala, Milan
1 February 1843
The action takes place in the city of Milan, and in the Holy Land, during 1096-7. Pagano, from Milan's ruling family, returns from exile after making an attempt on the life of his brother, Arvino. He repeats his crime, but accidentally kills his father instead. He is banished to the Holy Land, where he lives as a hermit in a cave near Antioch.
Several months later Lombard forces approach the city in the course of the First Crusade. Arvino's daughter Giselda, captured by the Muslims earlier in the campaign, falls in love with their leader's son, Oronte. He is killed in the final battle, in which the now reformed Pagano is also wounded after helping the Crusaders in their cause. As he dies in sight of the Holy City he is forgiven by Arvino and Giselda.

I LOMBARDI

ALLA PRIMA CROCIATA

DRAMMA LIRICO

DI TEMISTOCLE SOLERA

POSTO IN MUSICA

DAL SIG. MAESTRO GIUSEPPE VERDI

DA RAPPRESENTARSI

NELL' I. R. TEATRO ALLA SCALA

IL CARNEVALE MDCCCXLIII.

Milano

PER GASPARE TRUFFI

MDCCCXLIII

by the authorities. The new opera 'was a roaring success,' declared one critic. 'The common folk started to besiege the gallery from 3 o'clock onwards, bringing food with them so that the curtain rose amidst a strong smell of garlic sausages.'

The audience knew at once, of course, what the opera was really about: a crusade against the Austrians, and the liberation of Lombardo-Venetian territory. The great quintet in Act I, in which Lombard leaders are seen standing in the square in front of the basilica of San Ambrogio, pledged to a common cause, aroused the wildest enthusiasm and repeated demands for an encore, which the police in the theatre refused to allow. The great unison chorus O *Signore dal tetto natio* (O Lord from the land of our

A print published in
London in May 1846,
showing a scene from
the production of *I
Lombardi* at Her
Majesty's Theatre.

birth), which was inspired by a poem by Giusti, a young liberal writer,
sparked off riots in the streets of the city and, according to the critic
Dyneley Hussey, 'aroused the kind of fervour that *Land of our Fathers*
creates at a gathering of Welshmen'. He went on to say that the success of
the opera was, in fact, due more to its topicality than its artistic merit.

This view was shared by many of the critics of the time, who were
much less enthusiastic about *I Lombardi* than the public. When it was
produced in Venice in December of that year Verdi seems to have shared
some of their misgivings. In a letter to Giuseppina Appiani he described
the production as:

> . . . a great fiasco: one of the really classic fiascos. Everything was
> disapproved of, or just tolerated, with the exception of the *cabaletta*
> of the vision. That is the simple truth I relate to you with neither plea-
> sure nor sorrow.

Giuseppina Appiani, who was left with six children to rear after her
artist husband committed suicide, was another of Milan's celebrated
hostesses. It was in her salon in 1830 that Bellini composed most of *La
Sonnambula*, and Donizetti the whole of *Lucia di Lammermoor* in 1842.
Of all the composers who flourished immediately before Verdi, Donizetti
was the most influential: it was only after he left Milan that the younger
man became the principal musical celebrity in the Appiani household. In a
touching letter to Giuseppina Appiani, written from Bologna, Donizetti
confessed:

My heyday is over, and another must take my place. The world wants something new. Others have ceded their places to us and we must cede ours to still others . . . I am more than happy to give mine to people of talent like Verdi.

I Lombardi was the first of Verdi's operas to be performed in the USA. In 1847 the composer made substantial changes for a production at the Paris Opéra, and re-titled the piece *Jérusalem*. For reasons difficult to follow the Lombards became Franks and as a result all the powerful associations with the *Risorgimento*, which would have been received most sympathetically by a French audience, were completely lost. The amended version was greeted without much enthusiasm, and it was not until the unification and independence of Italy were achieved that I *Lombardi* in its original form was successfully revived.

With four operas behind him – the last two, overwhelming successes – was it Verdi's rather superstitious nature that led him to the conclusion that he dare not risk a fifth première at La Scala, or was he already dissatisfied with its falling standards of production? Whatever his reasons, and despite entreaties from the faithful Merelli, he decided to look elsewhere for his next commission. This was no problem since offers were now pouring in, among them a draft contract from the President of the Gran Teatro La Fenice in Venice. Two productions were required: an entirely new opera and a revival of *I Lombardi* to be ready for the next carnival season. Verdi haggled over the terms – he was now in a position to do so – not only about the fee he was to receive, but also over such important items as the choice of singers, librettists and subject matter.

He chose as his collaborator Francesco Maria Piave, a young poet with little experience of writing for the theatre, but whose way with words and willingness to learn made him an ideal junior partner for a musician of growing stature, confident in his own creative powers. Several topics had already been considered and rejected, including an operatic version of Shakespeare's *King Lear*, an idea that haunted Verdi for most of his career. After several false starts, he accepted a proposal from the theatre director to base his new opera on *Hernani*, a play by the French dramatist and novelist Victor Hugo. As soon as the authorities heard about this their

ERNANI
Teatro La Fenice, Venice
9 March 1844
The hero of the opera, set in 16th century Spain, is Ernani, a disgraced nobleman who has turned to banditry. He loves, and is loved by, Elvira. But she has been promised to a grandee, Silva, and has also caught the eye of Carlo, King of Spain, who places her under his protection. The affronted Silva challenges Ernani to a duel. Ernani asks for time so that he may first take his own revenge on Carlo. As a pledge he gives Silva a horn, promising that if he hears it at any time he will take his own life. Carlo is elected Emperor and, at Elvira's request, forgives his rivals, restores Ernani's property and gives his blessing to the marriage of the two lovers. But immediately after their wedding the sound of a horn is heard: Silva arrives and offers Ernani the option of poison or a dagger. Bound by his promise and his sense of duty and honour Ernani takes the dagger and stabs himself, as Silva gloats.

Francesco Maria Piave (1810-1876) wrote the libretti of several of Verdi's most famous operas, including *Rigoletto*, *La Traviata* and *La forza del destino*.

suspicions were aroused, for Hugo's play had caused a sensation when it was first produced in Paris. All the old classical conventions were overturned and the unities of time and space were ignored, much to the approval of the young *avant-garde*, who hailed the piece as an outstanding example of the new romantic drama then coming into fashion. To make matters worse, not only were the author's liberal views well-known but, to the horror of the censors, the plot of *Hernani* partly turns around a conspiracy against a crowned head. So it was regarded as highly dangerous and subversive stuff.

Verdi agreed to a number of changes and made others for his own musical purposes, much to the annoyance of Victor Hugo, who insisted that the opera must carry a different title to distinguish it from his own work. Thus *Ernani* came into being, and after a stormy period of preparation and rehearsal the composer's first new venture away from Milan was ready for the stage.

Even by the standards of the time this plot could not be more absurd or melodramatic. But, in comparison with *I Lombardi* with its eleven separate scenes or episodes, *Ernani* does have greater dramatic cohesion and the music a firmer sense of purpose and direction. The opera marks

Pauline Tinsley as Elvira and Robert Bickerstaff as Don Carlo in *Ernani* at Sadler's Wells Theatre, London, in 1967.

'an appreciable advance over Nabucco,' according to William Ashbrook, writing in *The Oxford Illustrated History of Opera*:

> There is a tightness of focus in the three men, the dashing outlaw (tenor), the predatory king (baritone), and the ruthless old noble (bass), each of whom wants Elvira (soprano) for himself, and their musical characterizations are sharp . . . . [The] terse but expressive final act of *Ernani* demonstrates Verdi's keen sense of musical theatre. Here he reached a level that he did not always maintain in his next few scores, although each minor work contains some signs of his unusual talent.

Like the other early operas, *Ernani* received a much more cordial reception from the public than from the more sober-minded critics. 'Organ-grinder's stuff,' sniffed Gounod. It was the work that extended Verdi's reputation beyond Italy's borders and was the first of his operas to be translated into English. Although not all authorities agree, *Ernani* has a strong claim to being the first opera to be recorded more or less complete. It came out in 1903 on forty single-sided ten inch discs, then recently introduced, and was issued by the Italian branch of the Gramophone and Typewriter Company.

Under the terms of his contract Verdi was obliged to conduct in person the first three performances at La Fenice in Venice, but he returned to Milan as soon as he could to deal with letters, invitations and other papers. As his fame spread and his commitments grew, administrative work took up a disproportionate amount of his time. His father-in-law, Antonio Barezzi, was quick to realize that he needed an assistant, so he sent a music student, Emanuele Muzio, to Milan. It was a replay of the composer's early years, for the young man had no money and, like Verdi, came from a village not far from Busseto. The arrangement was that he should act as general factotum in return for free music lessons. Despite his master's gruff, forbidding manner he became devoted to him and proved to be a capable and loyal assistant.

It was at this time that Verdi started a filing system [*Copialettere*] consisting of large scribbling books in which he kept copies of all important documents, letters and memoranda, many written in his own hand. These files were later maintained by Giuseppina Strepponi and form part of a vast archive that is still being studied. The lives and works of very few composers are so thoroughly documented, and it is a sombre thought that future scholars, working on the lives of leading composers of our own time, will have far fewer papers at their disposal. Telephone calls, fading faxes and other ephemeral means of communication have seen to that.

With his affairs in better order Verdi was able to turn his attention to the next commission, and chose an offer from Rome to provide an *opera di obbligo* for the start of the winter season at the Teatro Argentina in November 1844. He asked his librettist Piave to resume work on an earlier project *Lorenzino de' Medici*, but since this plot also concerns a regicide he prudently suggested an alternative based on Byron's play *The Two Foscari*. As he expected, the Roman police strongly objected to the first idea, and so work on *I due Foscari* began. Almost at once Verdi began to have doubts. The 'play does not have the theatrical grandeur needed for an opera,' he told Piave, 'so rack your brains and try to find something that will make a bit of a splash especially in the first act.' And later he urged him to 'take a good deal of trouble with it, because it is a fine subject, delicate and full of pathos.'

If the music of *I due Foscari* is less vigorous, less buoyant than the previous operas, it is much more atmospheric and depicts with greater subtlety of melodic line, harmony and of orchestration, the stress and emotional conflicts endured by each of the main characters. As the *Rivista di Romana* observed: 'Every protagonist speaks his own language; every character expresses his own feelings in a truly dramatic manner.'

The reactions of the first-night audience were favourable enough, although enthusiasm seems to have been tempered to some extent by an unwelcome rise in seat prices. For subsequent performances the normal rates applied, and the new opera was hailed as a masterpiece, with the composer taking no fewer than thirty curtain-calls on the second night.

While he was composing *I due Foscari* Verdi started to complain about headaches, stomach pains and a persistent sore throat, symptoms that reappeared whenever he was under stress, particularly creative stress. The

---

I DUE FOSCARI
Teatro Argentina, Rome
3 November 1844
In 1452 the Doge of Venice, Francesco Foscari, is forced to accept a decision taken by the Council of Ten to prolong the exile of his son, Jacopo, who is innocent of the murder of which he has been accused. Loredano, a member of the Council and an enemy of the Foscari family, rejects Jacopo's wife, Lucrezia, as she begs for mercy. Jacopo himself dies of a broken heart as the ship, on which he is held, sails out of the lagoon. The Council now demands the abdication of the Doge. At first he refuses, but then succumbs to their threats after ordering Loredano away from the ducal emblems. Malipiero is elected successor, as the broken old man sinks to the floor of the Council chamber and dies.

years in the galley were already taking their toll, but he allowed himself no respite.

Immediately on his return to Milan he started work on the next task, which was another opera for La Scala, possibly to compensate Merelli for the year in which he had allowed rival opera houses to share his output. Based on the story of Joan of Arc, as told by Schiller in his play *Die Jungfrau von Orleans*, and turned into a libretto by Solera, the score was completed in just under eight weeks and was made ready in great haste for its opening night. Schiller was not concerned with historical accuracy (for example, Joan dies in battle and not at the stake) but, as he explained to Goethe, he believed in the creation of symbols as a means of expressing poetic truth. Solera went further by having Joan fall in love with the French Dauphin rather than with Lionel, a handsome Englishman. This produces an effective trio for the Dauphin, Joan and her father, but makes nonsense of classical convention, the conflict between love and duty, which provides the impetus of the original drama.

Verdi seems not to have imposed the customary restraints on his librettist, nor to have burdened him with the usual number of helpful suggestions. This may have been because he was working under great pressure, but it is no less likely that the plot was of no interest to him. He preferred to work on subject-matter new to the operatic stage which had not passed through too many hands before his.

The patchy quality of Verdi's score is almost certainly due to the speed with which it was composed. It contains some of his finest music yet written, but at its worst it is 'provincial and childishly pretentious', in Julian Budden's memorable phrase. The loyal Muzio entertained no such doubts. The music 'will stun all the Milanese,' he declared in a letter back home to Busseto, with 'all sorts of music, the theatrical, the religious, the military.' It was an accurate enough forecast, for when *Giovanna d'Arco* was presented it was hailed as another worthy masterpiece by the young maestro.

But standards at La Scala were not what they had been, and tempers flared when Verdi discovered that Merelli was engaged in selling the rights of his new opera to Ricordi without his prior knowledge or authority. To make the situation worse, later in 1845 Merelli staged, without enlisting the composer's help, a revival of *I due Foscari* in which the second and third acts were presented in the wrong order. Verdi's fury can only be imagined: he vowed that never again would he compose for Merelli or for La Scala, an oath which he kept for twenty-five years.

Merelli's contract with La Scala came to an end the following year, 1846, and it was not until 1861 that he was re-appointed for a further term of two years. His departure from the scene removed any last traces of obligation Verdi may have felt towards the impresario personally, or to the opera house which had provided such crucial support earlier in his career.

Giuseppina Strepponi's few appearances in *Nabucco* at La Scala in 1842 marked the climax, but not the end of her professional career. After a year's complete rest she felt able to accept an invitation from the Teatro Ducale in Parma to appear once again in the leading role of Abigaille. In April 1843 Verdi came from Milan to stay with her for nearly two months, giving her the support and encouragement she needed during the

Charles, the French Dauphin, about to surrender to the invading English army in 1429, is dissuaded by Joan, a peasant girl whose heavenly voices have told her that she is to be the saviour of her country. Under her guidance and inspiration the French soldiers win an important battle, after which Charles declares his love for her. Joan responds, but explains that her voices have said that worldly love is not for her. Meanwhile, Joan's father, Giacomo, convinced that his daughter is in league with the Devil, first betrays her to the English and then, full of remorse, contrives her escape. However, in the next battle she receives a fatal wound and dies centre stage, standard in hand.

rehearsals, and conducting in person two of the twenty-two performances. It was a highly successful run, and Strepponi's delight may be imagined. Not only had she recovered something of her brilliant form as a singer, but she had at her side someone she greatly admired and whose company she enjoyed.

Verdi, for his part, continued to find her a much more agreeable and stimulating companion than the society hostesses and other ladies in Milan ready to throw themselves at his feet. He was a handsome, attractive and successful man, with plenty of admirers and would-be lovers, but as Gaia Servadio points out:

> Giuseppina showed him the value of good manners, coached him in languages, brought out a certain style that lay latent in Verdi; the grand ladies would never have taught him such things because they would have taken them for granted in him anyway.

It was not to be expected that their idyll in Parma would go unnoticed. Gossip soon spread, and the musical papers in Milan picked up the story, much to Verdi's annoyance. But Giuseppina allowed none of this to dim her happiness or her triumph. Two thousand people, including the Duchess Marie Louise, attended a benefit concert on 31 May, and a few days later, on the eve of her departure from Parma, she gave a charity concert free of charge to express her gratitude to the city.

Her next engagement was in Bologna, at the Teatro Communale, where the leading singer, Sofia Löwe, had been taken ill. Once again Giuseppina found herself playing Abigaille in *Nabucco*, but on this occasion a warning note was struck by the critic of *Il Figaro* who suggested that her voice 'was not what it had been earlier'. In January 1844 she sang in Verona; in May she gave a concert at the Teatro Regio in Turin; in August she appeared in Bergamo after which there followed an unhappy six-month season in Palermo.

Success awaited her once more in Alessandria and, later, in Modena, where she made her last appearance on the Italian operatic stage. In December 1845 there had been a calamitous performance of *I Lombardi*. Public outrage was so great that the police had to close the theatre, and the impresario sought to save his skin by hastily arranging a production of *Nabucco* with Strepponi as principal soloist. It was a heart-warming personal triumph for her: '. . . she took five curtain calls and even the ducal court showed clear signs of appreciation,' according to one local newspaper report.

With public order restored, the Modena management felt safe enough to put *I Lombardi* back into the programme, at which point the services of a *prima donna assoluta* of Giuseppina Strepponi's standing were, of course, no longer required. She sought other engagements, but without success.

Whenever his own commitments had allowed Verdi had joined Giuseppina during her travels: while they were in Bologna together they laid plans for her future. She knew, of course, that her singing career was almost at an end and that the only way she could pay off her remaining debts and earn a living in the future was to give lessons. She longed for retirement, but had the good sense to know that any dreams she had of spending the rest of her life with Verdi would have to wait: despite their deepening relationship the time was not yet ripe.

She was also clear-headed enough to realise that her best chance of making a fresh start was to go abroad, and so it was decided that she should set herself up as a singing teacher in Paris. Unlike Italy, which was in a state of political and economic upheaval, France had everything to offer – security, a stable economy, a vigorous and stimulating cultural life, flourishing opera houses and a growing interest in modern Italian opera, matched by a dearth of voices trained in the new, post *bel canto* style of singing.

Encouraged and assisted by Verdi, who arranged that Muzio should discreetly give her a series of lessons in harmony to fill one of the few gaps in her musical knowledge, she finally made up her mind to leave Italy. With her professional training and experience, her enquiring and lively mind, her artistry, her elegance, her social poise and natural dignity, success was hers for the asking. And if it were to prove possible for Verdi to be at her side, who could say what the future might hold? Not only the Opéra, but the whole of Paris, would surely be at their feet.

Chapter 5

Retreat to Recoaro

The citizens of Naples take great pride in their Teatro San Carlo for, as they will tell you, it has a tradition longer and richer than that of its two main rivals, La Scala and La Fenice. Earlier in the 19th century, when Rossini wrote nine of his greatest operas in seven years, the San Carlo had one of the best orchestras and the finest singers to be found anywhere in Italy. Standards remained high, and when the impresario Vincenzo Flauto offered Verdi a commission within two weeks of the spectacular success of

Salvatore Cammarano (1801-1852), the most celebrated librettist of the period, came from a large theatrical family in Naples. He worked with Verdi on a number of operas, including *Il Trovatore*, and wrote the libretto of *Lucia di Lammermoor* by Donizetti.

Teatro San Carlo, Naples
12 August 1845
The action takes place in Peru in the middle years of the 16th century.
An Inca chief, Zamoro, has been tortured by the Christians. When he gets back to his tribe he finds that his betrothed, Alzira, has been seized by Gusmano, the local Spanish governor. Zamoro sets out to rescue Alzira but is captured once again: in desperation she agrees to marry Gusmano to secure Zamoro's release. But his guards have already been bribed and, disguised in Spanish uniform, he arrives at the wedding to kill Gusmano with a hidden dagger. In a dying gesture Gusmano forgives his attacker and prays that he and Alzira may live together in peace and happiness.

A carefully posed photograph of the composer, in pensive mood, taken in 1845.

Ernani in Venice, the composer lost no time in getting down to negotiations. Before starting work on *Giovanna d'Arco* he clearly set out terms for a new opera in his usual shrewd and business-like manner. One of the attractions of a contract in Naples was the opportunity of working with the resident poet Salvatore Cammarano, then regarded as the most gifted of all Italian librettists. He had written the text *of Lucia di Lammermoor* and other great Donizetti successes, and was adroit at evading the censors whose activities in Naples were more repressive than elsewhere in Italy.

Verdi and Cammarano chose Voltaire's play *Alzira* for their first collaboration. It was an unusual choice since the play is more concerned with ideas than with action: religion and politics are discussed at some length, and there is a great deal of dialogue. However, little or no trace of all this can be found in Cammarano's libretto.

Terms were agreed readily enough, but illness intervened. Verdi found it impossible to keep to his original schedule; the headaches, digestive troubles and sore throat, almost certainly stress disorders, recurred, and he was ordered to rest. Vincenzo Flauto foolishly suggested that doses of wormwood and the air of Vesuvius would soon effect a cure. He had yet to learn that one does not make light-hearted remarks on such matters to a person of Verdi's temperament or standing. He received a sharp reply to the effect that wormwood and Vesuvius would not 'get all my functions working again.' 'Quiet and rest are required', said the composer firmly: in a separate letter to Cammarano he complained that 'we artists apparently are not allowed to be ill.'

Reports vary on the reaction of the San Carlo audience to the new opera. After the opening night Verdi said that 'It is a success as great as that of *Ernani*', but many years later he described *Alzira* as a 'really dreadful work', redeemed only by the finales to the two acts and by the overture. A few months after it was first performed in Naples the opera was presented in Rome, where the reception was also lukewarm. But by this time Verdi had put the failure behind him and had already focused his attention on his next commission. This came not from an opera house but from a publisher, Francesco Lucca, who was Ricordi's main competitor in Milan. In a letter to his friend Jacopo Ferretti, who wrote the libretto of Rossini's *La Cenerentola*, Verdi said, 'I am at present at work on *Attila*. What a fine subject! The critics can say what they like, but I say what a beautiful musical libretto!'

In the spring of 1884 the composer had read Zacharias Werner's play

ATTILA
Teatro La Fenice, Venice
17 March 1846
Odabella, daughter of the Lord of Aquileia, an Italian city north of Rome captured by Attila the Hun in 452, offers false loyalty to the invader while at the same time plotting to kill him in revenge for her father's death. Foresto, her lover, agrees to help her and tries to poison Attila, who heeds an omen not to proceed with his attack on Rome. Odabella, determined to kill Attila herself, warns him of the danger and demands the release of Foresto as her reward. Attila agrees, but claims Odabella as his future bride. Foresto and others now doubt her loyalty, but in the final scene she plunges a dagger into Attila's heart.

Attila, König der Hunnen (*Attila*, King of the Huns) which had impressed him a great deal. He made a note of the name, adding it others he had already jotted down as possible subjects for future operas. Again, it was a surprising choice for Werner's work inhabits an alien Wagnerian world as far removed from the warmth, the passion and the colour of Italy as it is possible to imagine. But when Verdi agreed to write an opera for Lucca, *Attila* was the idea that came forward. Once again, Piave was told to sharpen his pen, but Solera also became involved. Much of the final libretto was his work, and Piave was left to make the odd contribution to the text here and there.

Librettists had plenty of duties other than the writing of words, for it was their job to organise the costumes and the scenery within the budgets laid down by the theatre management, and to direct the movements of the soloists and chorus on stage. Producers did not make their appearance in the Italian theatre until the 1850s. In France, at the Paris Opéra, very detailed production books were kept giving precise instructions on such matters as movement, scenery and costume: these were of value when staging revivals or mounting repertory items.

Solera took even greater liberties with Werner than Cammarano had taken with Voltaire. Moreover, he left his work unfinished in order to follow his *prima donna* wife on a visit to Spain. Verdi took all this with uncharacteristic resignation: he was still in poor health and had lost something of his earlier resilience and bite. The two men were agreed that *Attila* should have a strong patriotic element – the prologue contains the stirring line *Avrai tu l'universo, resti Italia a me* (Take the whole universe, but leave Italy to me) – but the composer resisted Solera's plan to have a choral finale in the grand manner. The row that followed brought to an end the collaboration that had worked so well up to that time. It is almost certainly true, as Julian Budden suggests, that Verdi 'had outgrown Solera's ideas of musical theatre'.

Muzio had great difficulty extracting the libretto from Solera. During one of his many visits he was furious to find the 'lazy dog hasn't done a thing . . . this morning at eleven o'clock he was still in bed.' But if the librettist had delivered the text on time it is unlikely that Verdi would have been able to do much with it, for he had succumbed to a severe nervous depression as a result of taking on too many commitments. In a mood of self-pity he thanked one of his correspondents . . .

Raffaele Arie and Marcella Roberti in the 1964 revival of *Attila* at the Teatro dell'Opera, Rome.

. . . for remembering your poor friend condemned continually to scribble musical notes. God saves the ears of every good Christian from having to listen to them! Accursed notes!

Uncertain health and Solera's delays meant that not much of the score of *Attila* was ready for production by the time Verdi arrived in Venice in December 1845. His attempts to make up for lost time were interrupted by bouts of gastric fever, one of which confined him to bed for three weeks. Lucca proved no more sympathetic than Flauto had before him: the stricken composer complained about his 'most irritating and ungrateful manner' and that 'he forced me to complete *Attila* in a deplorable physical condition.' Recalling the crisis four years later Verdi wrote 'when I was almost dying I gave my word to finish *Attila*, and I did so.' Despite all the difficulties, the opening night, delayed until 17 March 1846, proved to be another huge success. After the performance he wrote to the Countess Maffei:

The applause and the calls were too much for a poor sick man. Perhaps it was not completely understood, but it may be this evening. My friends would say that this is the best of my operas; the public questions that; I say that it is not inferior to the others; time will decide.

Time has decided, and on the whole its verdict has gone against both *Alzira* and *Attila*. The distinguished critic Francis Toye was not alone when he dismissed *Alzira* as the worst of all Verdi operas; Charles Osborne finds it 'unsatisfactory and naïve, though it contains much excellent and beautiful music'; Julian Budden assures us that 'No Verdi opera is totally negligible,' and offers the little-known fact that a generation later it inspired the Brazilian composer Carlos Gomes to write his major work, *Il Guarany*. Verdi himself admitted in a letter to Count Maffei that he wrote the opera 'without any great care or much exertion, so that if it fails I shan't mind very much.'

Attempts to revive the piece include productions at the Teatro dell' Opera, Rome, in 1967, and later at Covent Garden in the 1980s. But these have met only with limited success, and it is difficult to avoid the conclusion that if *Alzira* had not been written by Verdi but by another composer, less famous and less gifted, it would by now have been completely forgotten, and the parts left to moulder in an unknown provincial opera house.

Attila is a different matter. Some of the music has a grandeur that recalls the finest moments in *Nabucco*, and there are other passages of great delicacy and beauty. With the exception of Odabella, a character so inconsistent as to be beyond belief, the principal parts are well realized and the latent nobility of *Attila* as the barbarian undone by treachery is convincingly portrayed.

The none-too-subtle calls on Venetian city pride and Italian national feeling could hardly fail to draw an immediate, overwhelming response from audiences all over the country. The censors tried in vain to impose control, but they knew that if they insisted on the removal of 'provocative' parts of the text or threatened to close the theatre, the audience would take their protest to the streets and stage demonstrations. In the pre-revolutionary mood of the times it was decided that exhibitions of patriotic enthusiasm were less dangerous indoors than outside, where matters might get out of hand and damage be done to persons and property.

However, years later, when the objects of the *Risorgimento* had been largely achieved and political turmoil had subsided, calls for freedom and national unity became less relevant and were increasingly seen as rather obvious devices to win audience support and approval. So the opera lost impact and the popularity it had enjoyed in its heyday started to wane. Also, of course, as time passed audiences were able to compare the earlier operas with the later masterpieces: who would want to see *Attila* when *Rigoletto*, *La Traviata* or *Il Trovatore* were on offer?

For these reasons *Attila* eventually disappeared from the repertoire. The strength of its patriotic sentiment contains the seed of its principal weakness and, unlike *Nabucco* or *I Lombardi*, the musical and dramatic qualities are such that the work has not yet figured in the recent revival of interest in early Verdi operas. Benjamin Lumley, the manager of Her Majesty's Theatre in London, entertained no such doubts when *Attila* first appeared. 'None perhaps of Verdi's works,' he said, 'has kindled so much enthusiasm in Italy or crowned the fortunate composer with more abundant laurels . . .' During rehearsals he engaged Verdi to write an opera for London, and it was only illness that prevented the contract being fulfilled. By January the composer's diet was restricted to boiled milk and water, and two months later his doctors certified that he was quite unable to travel. Yet again it was suggested that a change of climate would prove beneficial, and Lumley urged the composer 'to come as soon as possible to try the good remedy I propose.' But Verdi sent his regrets and with his

In 1831 Giuseppe Mazzini (1805-1872), exiled in Marseilles, founded the Young Italy movement to unify the country under republican government. In 1849 he was one of a triumvirate during the short-lived Roman republic, but after its collapse his influence waned.

friend Count Maffei retired to the spa town of Recoaro, near Lake Garda in the foothills of the Dolomites, where he rested and took the waters.

It was not in Verdi's nature, however, to remain idle for long and within weeks he accepted an invitation from the manager of the Teatro della Pergola in Florence to compose an opera for the 1847 season. From three possible subjects he chose *Macbeth*, partly because Lanari, the Florentine impresario, was able to provide a reliable baritone for the title role, and partly because Maffei shared the composer's long-standing admiration for the works of Shakespeare. 'This tragedy is one of the greatest creations of man . . .', wrote Verdi in a letter to his librettist Piave. 'If we can't make something great out of it let us at least try to do something out of the ordinary.'

Such admiration is the more remarkable when it is remembered that Verdi's knowledge of Shakespearean drama rested entirely on prose or verse translations in French or Italian, some of indifferent quality and literary merit. As we know, he often returned to the idea of basing an

MACBETH
Teatro della Pergola, Florence
14 March 1847
In the opera the setting and outline of Shakespeare's plot are kept, but much subsidiary action and many minor characters are discarded. Macbeth and his fellow-general Banquo are confronted by a group of witches, who prophesy that he will reign, but that the kingdom will eventually pass into the hands of Banquo's descendants. The ruthlessly ambitious Lady Macbeth persuades her husband to kill King Duncan while their guest, and arranges to have Banquo killed to remove any threat to the succession.

However, the consciences of both are aroused by their bloody crimes. The ghost of Banquo appears at a banquet and Macbeth's guilt is revealed to the guests. The witches repeat their forecast that Banquo's heirs will succeed. Lady Macbeth walks in her sleep, haunted by images of Duncan and bloodshed. Refugees led by Macduff are joined by an army commanded by Malcolm, Duncan's son. At the castle of Dunsinane Lady Macbeth dies and the terror-stricken Macbeth learns of the approach of the rebels carrying branches from Birnam Wood. In the battle he is killed, and Malcolm proclaimed the new King.

opera on the very difficult text of *King Lear*. When he embarked on *Macbeth* he had not seen a Shakespeare play on stage, even in translation. What Verdi wanted for his musical theatre, according to Harold Powers, Professor of Music at Princeton University, was 'not a drama for which he would provide background music, but a play that could be made, to use his own expression, *musicabile*. Like so many musicians and writers of the time, Verdi held Shakespeare as 'the rallying point of Continental Romanticism,' to quote Harold Powers once more:

> The contrast of the grotesque and tragic . . . was embodied for him in Shakespeare, whom he regularly cited as the antithesis of the classical unities of the *grand siècle*, the . . . monotony of affect and effect.

Verdi recognised that the main characters in the opera are Macbeth, Lady Macbeth and the Witches. In the foreshortening that takes place when reducing a stage play rich in vocabulary and powerful imagery to a libretto, subtleties and colourful details in the original text are inevitably lost. The character to suffer most in the operatic version is that of Macbeth himself, for he becomes a villain without depth, a figure too flatly-drawn. On the other hand, Lady Macbeth is wonderfully portrayed: hers is almost certainly the greatest soprano role from all the pre-*Rigoletto* operas. The music given to the witches is less convincing: a relentless forward momentum conveys their pent-up energy and shrill orchestral effects might be said to reflect their malice, but nowhere does Verdi conjure up the weird terror and sense of doom that Berlioz, for example, so vividly expresses.

Other choral writing varies in quality. The banality of the chorus for Banquo's murderers beggars description and, as Dyneley Hussey points out, it has been made 'for ever ridiculous by Sullivan's parody ('With cat-like tread') in *The Pirates of Penzance*. The famous *brindisi* or drinking song in Act II looks rather commonplace on the page but proves effective enough in performance, especially when it comes second time round as Lady Macbeth tries to reassure the guests after Banquo's ghost terrifies her husband.

The chorus of Scottish exiles at the beginning of Act IV was one of the pieces completely re-written for a new production in Paris given in April 1865, the version by which we know the opera today. It is more than another routine evocation of patriotic sentiment in the *Va, pensiero* mould. With its daring harmonies and striking orchestration the music is a foretaste of the Verdi yet to come – the Verdi of the *Requiem* and the even more innovative *Four Sacred Pieces*.

Among other strikingly original and powerful passages in the original version are the 'dagger' scene in Act I, the duet between Macbeth and his wife and the later sleep-walking scene, all of which Verdi wisely left untouched. In a much-quoted letter the composer explains how he wants the role of Lady Macbeth to be performed:

Tadolini, I believe, is to sing Lady Macbeth, and I am astonished that she should have undertaken the part. You know how highly I regard Tadolini, and she herself knows it, but for the sake of us all I must say this to you: Tadolini's qualities are much too fine for this role. This may seem to you absurd, but Tadolini has a beautiful and attractive figure, and I want Lady Macbeth to be ugly and evil. Tadolini sings to perfection, and I don't want Lady Macbeth to sing at all. Tadolini has a wonderful voice, clear, flexible, strong, while Lady Macbeth's voice should be hard, stifled and dark. Tadolini's voice is angelic; I want Lady Macbeth's to be diabolic. . . . the two most important numbers in the opera are the duet between Lady Macbeth and her husband, and the Sleepwalking Scene. If these two numbers fail, then the entire opera fails. And these numbers must definitely not be sung: they must be acted and declaimed in a voice hollow and veiled otherwise the effect will be lost. The orchestra *muted*.

Verdi was certainly not lacking in experience when dealing with quick-tempered and temperamental Italian singers. He wanted to make sure they had their sights fixed on the dramatic quality of their roles, without allowing that quality to become subordinated in any way to the music. He goes on to explain, among other things, how the stage should be set and how the apparitions should appear, for by the time he wrote his letter to Cammarano (23 November 1848) the composer had taken the opportunity of seeing a production of Shakespeare's play during his stay in London and now considered himself well-qualified to offer advice on such matters. When he finished *Macbeth* in its original form Verdi had no doubts about its stature. In a letter to his father-in-law, Barezzi, he said:

For a long time I have had it in mind to dedicate a work to you, who have been to me a father, a benefactor and a friend . . . Here, then, is *Macbeth*, which I love above all my other works and for that reason deem it most worthy to be presented to you.

The first night in Florence went moderately well, but after the second performance Verdi was cheered by a wildly enthusiastic audience, some of whom insisted on accompanying him through the city streets as he walked back to his apartment. The following year, at the San Carlo and at La Fenice the opera was equally well received.

However, as the years passed it was neglected, and the revival at the Théâtre Lyrique in Paris eighteen years later did little to restore the work to public favour. Verdi adjusted some of the harmonisation and orchestration and to cater for Parisian tastes he wrote some ballet music, now very rarely performed.

Lady Macbeth's great soliloquy *La luce langue* (Daylight is fading), is among the later additions, and became one of the most awe-inspiring scenes in the whole opera. Verdi virtually created his own text, taking as his inspiration Macbeth's lines:

Light thickens; and the crow
Makes wing to th' rooky wood . . .

The 1865 version of the opera is the one we hear today, although many years were to pass before it became fully part of the repertoire. It was not heard in England, for example, until 1936 when it was first produced at Glyndebourne. To a generation that regards this revised *Macbeth* as one of the most important of the pre-*Rigoletto* operas, such long neglect is difficult to understand.

Chapter 6

Standards Raised: Standards Lowered

As Verdi's health continued to improve he was ready, by November 1846, to follow up Benjamin Lumley's invitation to write a new opera for Her Majesty's Theatre in London. The terms offered were generous, and to have his first premiere outside Italy in so famous a venue was an opportunity he could not afford to miss. He had intended to take Byron's *The Corsair* as his subject, but found Piave's libretto 'dull and lacking in theatrical effectiveness.' In its place he chose a text based on Schiller's play *Die Räuber*, that Maffei had started during their work together on *Macbeth*. This was the proposal he now put to Lumley on condition that the celebrated Swedish soprano Jenny Lind, who had taken London by storm, would be engaged to play the principal role of Amalia.

I masnadieri (The Robbers) lacks the stature of *Macbeth* or *Nabucco*, and is of interest mainly because this is the work in which, for the first time, Verdi succeeds in presenting a convincingly evil male character, Francesco. He is the first in a long line of malevolent villains that reaches ultimate fulfilment in the Iago of *Otello*.

So brief a summary of the plot cannot convey its complexity. Maffei was an accomplished poet but, unlike the brutal Solera or the mild-mannered Piave, he was no librettist. Verdi had harried Piave without mercy over *Macbeth*, yet he gave a free hand to Maffei with *I masnadieri*.

Did he have a false idea of the Count's abilities or did he hesitate to criticise the work of someone he regarded, even now, as his social superior? For whatever reason his failure to supervise the text is clearly evident: he had to write music for 'a succession of indigestible dramatic

---

I MASNADIERI
Her Majesty's Theatre, London
22 July 1847
Francesco, son of Count Massimiliano, intrigues against his elder brother Carlo to gain his inheritance. Carlo flees the family castle (which, despite the Italian-sounding names of the principal characters, is set in 18th century Germany) and becomes leader of a robber band. Francesco pretends that his brother is dead and pays court to Amalia, the orphan niece of Count Massimiliano. She remains faithful to her beloved Carlo who, after burning down a city to rescue a comrade, returns in disguise to rescue his father, now imprisoned by Francesco and close to death by starvation. Meanwhile, Amalia has been taken captive. Overcome by grief and guilt Carlo stabs her, crying to the robbers as he does so, 'I sacrifice an angel to you.'

units', as Julian Budden puts it. However much he may have kept his own counsel Verdi was probably aware of the limitations of his collaborator, for *I masnadieri* was the last project on which the two men worked together.

In May 1847 Verdi and Muzio set off from Milan. On reaching Paris by a somewhat roundabout and leisurely route, Muzio went on ahead to arrange accommodation in London and to ensure, contrary to rumours they had heard, that Jenny Lind was prepared to learn a new part and to take on the challenging role of Amalia. Verdi probably stayed with Giuseppina Strepponi during his few days in Paris and certainly visited the Opéra where, according to a letter to the Countess Maffei, he 'never heard more awful singers or a more mediocre chorus.' In London he found the smell of coal smoke upsetting, although his small suite was 'quite clean, like all the houses . . .' The letter continues:

I can't tell you how fanatical they are about Lind. They are already selling boxes and seats for tomorrow evening. I can't wait to hear her.

Six weeks later, on 17 July 1847, he wrote again to the Countess:

You will be surprised to hear I am still in London, and that the opera has not yet been staged. The smoke and the fog are to blame, as well as this diabolical climate, which robs me of all desire to work . . . I have had two orchestral rehearsals, and if I were in Italy I would know by now whether the work was good or not, but here I understand nothing. Blame the climate . . . blame the climate!

In other respects Verdi's stay was less disagreeable. As soon as he was seen at Her Majesty's Theatre he was warmly welcomed by the public and the press, and was invited to attend dinners and other social events. He enjoyed the countryside around London and liked the people he met.

The premiere of *I masnadieri* was a glittering social occasion attended by Her Majesty Queen Victoria, who later wrote in her diary that she found the music 'very noisy and trivial.' The Prince Consort was also present, together with Prince Louis Bonaparte, the future Emperor of France who had recently escaped from imprisonment, the Duke of Cambridge and other leading figures. According to the *Morning Post*, when Verdi was first seen in the orchestra pit 'there was continuous applause which went on for a quarter of an hour', and at the end of the performance he was again loudly cheered by the audience.

Not for the first time in Verdi's career some critics shared the enthusiasm of the first-night audience, others did not. Henry Fothergill Chorley said in *The Athenaeum* that this 'is the worst opera that has been given in our time at Her Majesty's Theatre. Verdi is finally rejected.' Other notices were no less hostile and at the performance on the second night, which Verdi also conducted, the audience was perceptibly cooler. Unperturbed, the ever-loyal Muzio wrote:

Verdi aroused a *furore* in London but the English are a matter-of-fact and thoughtful people and never give way to enthusiasm like the Italians, partly because they can't understand too well, and partly because they think that well-bred people shouldn't make a lot of noise.'

A contemporary engraving showing the auditorium of Her Majesty's Theatre in London.

Two more performances before the end of the season at Her Majesty's Theatre were followed by a few productions in Italy, but despite being translated into a number of European languages the opera soon dropped out of the repertoire. At one point Lumley tried to retain Verdi's services but the composer set such a high price on them, probably deliberately, that no agreement could be reached. By the end of July, having sent Muzio back to Milan, Verdi returned to Paris.

The plans so carefully prepared in Bologna were bearing fruit. A life shared with Giuseppina and a commission from the Paris Opéra were twin objectives now firmly within his grasp. Writing to Luigi Toccagni from Paris he says:

> After all, here I enjoy the individual freedom that I have always desired and never have been able to attain. I visit no-one, no-one knows me and I do not have the inconvenience of being pointed out, as in so many cities in Italy. I enjoy good health, I write a good deal, affairs are going well . . .

Again, it would be wise to make some allowances for Verdi's sense of drama because the picture he paints, or at least suggests, of a life of solitary bliss is not really supported by the facts. The capable Giuseppina took her responsibilities seriously and as lady of the house saw to it that there were plenty of interesting guests for Verdi to meet at dinner parties and on other occasions. Her social skills, her wit and her knowledge of the world made her an excellent hostess; Verdi's social and musical interests could not have been in better hands.

He had made it clear to the management of the Paris Opéra that there was not time to produce a new work but, following precedent, he would reshape an earlier opera, *I Lombardi*, altering the plot and writing new music as required. Two poets responsible for the text of Donizetti's *La Favorite*, Alphonse Royer and Gustave Vaëz, were commissioned to prepare a new libretto, and Verdi settled down to write a score which, on completion, differed a great deal from the original version. Some critics believe that *Jérusalem*, as the revised work is known, with its tauter, more believable plot and better-crafted linking musical passages, is the finer work. But it is now rarely performed, unlike *I Lombardi* which nowadays is occasionally staged.

The first performance of *Jérusalem*, at the Académie Royale de Musique in Paris on 22 November 1847, was a success. The first two acts were later presented by royal command at Les Tuileries. On this occasion Verdi was created a Chevalier of the Légion d'Honneur by the 'Citizen King' Louis-Philippe, whose hold on the French throne was becoming increasingly precarious in the face of republican sentiment, growing in France as in the rest of Europe. To these honours were added handsome financial rewards, since Verdi had insisted that his fee should not be reduced: an adaptation was no less valuable than an entirely original work. He also negotiated the sale of Italian rights to Ricordi in a version entitled *Gerusalemme* to be dedicated to Giuseppina Strepponi.

There could be no clearer indication of the strengthening of the bond between them. She was with him as he laboured on the score: at one point, in a new love duet, her handwriting actually appears on the page. Intuitively she knew when to offer suggestions; when to praise and encourage; when to criticise and when to lapse into a companionable silence. As a creative artist herself she understood completely his way of working, a matter on which the composer himself throws light in a fascinating letter to Umberto Giordano, a young colleague of Mascagni and composer of *Andrea Chenier*:

. . . never correct what you wrote on the previous day – you will not like it any more and you will mistakenly destroy all that you have done. Compose the first act, without pausing, without corrections; when you have done this, put the sheets of music to one side and start the second act. Proceed with the second act in exactly the same way, and then continue with the third and fourth acts. Then rest. When you have recovered your strength, revise and correct everything: you can be sure that this is the only way of avoiding error . . . Work every day, at any work to hand – without daily exercise the hand . . . grows stiff. Never read newspaper reviews after a premiere and never pay homage to journalists with your visiting card.

Soon after Christmas 1847 Antonio Barezzi came to Paris to consult his son-in-law on various questions concerning property in Busseto, and was immediately captivated by 'La Signora Peppina'. He was not unaware, of course, of her earlier reputation, but her kindness towards him, her charm, consideration and, not least, her obvious devotion to Verdi, won his warm admiration. On his return home nothing he could say or do could stem the flood of vindictive gossip still circulating in Milan about Verdi and his

> **IL CORSARO**
> Teatro Grande, Trieste
> 25 October 1848
> A pirate captain, Corrado, is captured while leading an attack on the Turkish leader, Pasha Seid. He in turn is killed by a favourite slave, Gulnara, who frees Corrado and begs him to take her with him to his island. However, on his return Corrado finds that his true love, Medora, believing him to be dead, has taken poison. She dies in his arms and the grief-stricken Corsair plunges into the sea and is drowned.

mistress, but at least he had the satisfaction of seeing for himself that theirs was not a casual or ill-considered relationship.

Verdi had planned to return to Milan by February 1848, but 'a slight temperature and a cold' made him delay his departure. There was also a disagreeable obligation to be met, for he had not yet sent off the last of the three operas he had undertaken to compose for the 'tiresome and indelicate' Lucca, with whom he was now on extremely bad terms. Verdi blamed him for standing in the way of more lucrative engagements, which was untrue, and was furious when Lucca suggested subjects other than *The Corsair*. For it was to Piave's libretto, which he had so roundly criticised, that he had returned and set to music with scarcely a line changed. Verdi's insistence on using Byron's romantic poem was well-judged, for it had gained great popularity throughout Italy.

Il corsaro has moments of great lyrical beauty and depth of feeling, but much of the chorus work is uninspired, and the unfolding of the plot entirely predictable. Perhaps his irritation with Lucca explains such short-comings, but Verdi appears to have shown very little interest in the composition or the production of this opera, which he left entirely in the hands of Muzio, or in its subsequent fate.

Lucca decided to stage the first performance at the Teatro Grande in Trieste, but this had to be delayed until the autumn of 1848 on account of the political turmoil. When the opera did at last appear on 25th October it was severely mauled by the public and the press. After only three performances it was withdrawn.

In February 1848 Verdi finally made up his mind to return to Milan, only to discover that obstacles far more serious than high temperatures and colds now stood in his path. Social and political unrest, fermenting for many months, suddenly erupted. The people of Paris took to the barricades, Louis-Philippe was deposed, and within two days the Second Republic was proclaimed. These dramatic events were part of a wider pattern of revolt; Bourbon rule had already been overthrown in Palermo; in March there was an uprising in Vienna, the capital of the Austrian Empire, which was followed by armed rebellion in Venice and Lombardy.

'Now it is our turn,' wrote Verdi to a friend in Milan on 11 February 1848. Prophetic words, for a month later the Milanese rose against their Austrian masters who, after five days of bitter fighting (the glorious *Cinque Giornate*) were driven out of the city. A notable heroine of the revolt was Princess Belgiojoso, a friend of Giuseppina Strepponi. Mounted on a white horse, wearing a plumed hat and flourishing the Italian tricolour, she led a private army of 160 men in an attack on the ramparts of the Porta Romana, one of the main gates. 'The crowds watched her from the barricades and the piazzas,' writes Gaia Servadio, 'with the stupe-faction of an audience at La Scala.'

Verdi reached Milan after the battle, and was immediately asked to become a tribune. However, he was dismayed to find disunity, jealous in-fighting and jockeying for political position among the leaders of the revolution, in all of which he was determined to play no part. Bitterly dis-appointed by the turn of events he made his way back to Paris, but not before purchasing a large house just outside Busseto, near his birthplace, called the Villa Sant'Agata.

A third ambition fulfilled.

Muddle and stalemate prevailed in northern Italy until July 1848, when the Austrian field marshal Radetsky, of Radetsky March fame, attacked the rebels and forced them to withdraw. Verdi signed a petition seeking the help of the French commander-in-chief, who regretfully explained that with his hands full dealing with domestic unrest he could not possibly come to the aid of a sister republic. An armistice was signed, and Milan was re-occupied by Austrian troops.

Verdi continued to keep a close eye on the situation, but he could not allow his career to lose momentum. He assumed, wrongly as it transpired, that the balance of his contract with the Teatro San Carlo had lapsed after a change of management. While he was glad to be free of a tedious commitment, some other source of income had to be found. He turned his attention to a project he had been nursing for some time: a new opera for Ricordi to be produced anywhere in Italy except La Scala and, most importantly, with Cammarano as the librettist. An idea based on Bulwer Lytton's *The Last of the Tribunes* did not go down well with Cammarano,

Street fighting in Milan during the 1848 uprising.

Villa Sant'Agata.

who countered with a proposal that they should use a plot by the French dramatist-poet Joseph Méry, set in the Peninsular War, changing time and place to feature the victory won by the Lombard League against the Emperor Barbarossa in 1176. It was agreed that this was a suitably patriotic theme. A title was chosen, *La battaglia di Legnano*, and work began – but very slowly, for Cammarano was his own man and not one to be hurried.

'A story like that', declared the librettist, 'should stir every man with an Italian soul in his breast.' How right he was.

Work on *La battaglia di Legnano* did not proceed smoothly during the remaining months of 1848 as frequent letters addressed to Cammarano reveal. 'If you had not imposed two months indolence upon me without sending me one word of text, I should by now have finished this opera,' Verdi complained in September, following this a few days later with a further plea.

LA BATTAGLIA DI LEGNANO
Teatro Argentina, Rome
27 January 1849
Arrigo, a soldier from Verona, is wounded in battle and returns home only to find that during his absence Lida, his betrothed, has married a Milanese army captain, Rolando. When the German Emperor, Frederico Barbarossa, invades Italy the disconsolate hero joins the Knights of Death, whose members are sworn to die in the defence of Milan. Lida begs him to change his mind, but they are discovered together by Rolando who bitterly denounces them. In the battle that follows Arrigo kills Barbarossa but is himself mortally wounded. His dying testimony to Rolando is that Lida is 'guiltless and as pure as an angel'. He dies with the Lombardian standard to his lips as the final chorus swells to an impressive patriotic climax.

Cammarano's delays, however, did allow the composer to honour a promise he had made to the rebel leader Mazzini for a setting of a patriotic poem, *Suona la tromba*, written by a young revolutionary poet, Goffredo Mameli. In a covering letter Verdi expressed the hope that the hymn 'may soon be sung on the plains of Lombardy, amid the music of the cannon.' Sadly, his gesture came too late, for by the time the score reached Mazzini the fighting in Lombardy had been over for some months.

Elsewhere in Italy the political cauldron remained on the boil. In Rome the papal administrator Count Rossi was murdered by a Republican extremist and the Pope was forced to take refuge in the coastal town of Gaeta, outside Vatican jurisdiction. Free elections were called but from his place of exile His Holiness imposed a ban on Catholics taking part: this measure proved to be a gross error of judgement since it enabled the Republicans to win with a huge majority.

By the time Verdi arrived in the city to supervise rehearsals of *La battaglia di Legnano* it was widely assumed that the new Assembly would declare the Papal State a republic at its inaugural meeting in February. Well before the start of the first performance on 27 January 1849, excitement in the crowded theatre was at fever pitch. The impressive overture opens with a march-like motif associated with the Lombard League which, to British ears at least, bears a close resemblance to the signature tune used for the successful television series *Z-Cars*. The motif is repeated in the opening chorus to cries of *Viva Italia*!, and when this point in the score was reached the effect on that first-night audience in Rome, passions already inflamed, was overwhelming. To every *Viva Italia!* from the stage came cries of *Viva Italia!* and *Viva Verdi!* from the audience. Later in the opera, when Arrigo leaps from a balcony to rejoin his regiment a soldier, fired by his example, flung his topcoat from one of the boxes and then threw onto the stage all the chairs he could lay hands on until he was restrained by the *carabinieri*.

Wild with enthusiasm, the crowd refused to let the singers leave the stage at the end of the performance: the short, rousingly patriotic final act had to be repeated in its entirety. This became an instant tradition which was observed at all subsequent performances in Rome, much to the discomfiture of the Austrian censors. Before the opera could be performed in any other Italian opera house they insisted the setting be changed to the Netherlands and the title altered to *L'Assedio di Arlem*, (The Siege of Harlem).

The subsequent history of this remarkable work which, although written very much in the grand manner, shows a subtlety of technique only rarely to be found among its predecessors, is not dissimilar to the fate that overtook other overtly nationalistic and patriotic operas from Verdi's early period. Much of their force and much of the popular appeal were lost when Italy finally threw off the Austrian yoke. Until fairly recently, revivals have been few and far between. In the case of *La battaglia di Legnano* one of the more remarkable of these was *The Battle* given in Cardiff in October 1960 under the direction of Sir Charles Groves, a production set in northern Italy at the time of the German occupation during World War II.

While Verdi was working on *La battaglia di Legnano* the management of the Teatro San Carlo woke up to the fact that he still owed them an

LUISA MILLER
Teatro San Carlo, Naples
8 December 1849

The heroine, the daughter of an old soldier, falls in love with Rodolfo whom she assumes to be a commoner like herself. But his father, Count Walther, is determined that Rodolfo shall marry Federica, Duchess of Ostheim. Together with Wurm, his evil steward, Walther plots to separate the lovers. He has Luisa's father arrested and forces her to write a letter saying that it is not Rodolfo she loves but Wurm. Once free, Luisa's father plans to go into exile with his daughter, but Rodolfo arrives and, together with Luisa, drinks wine he has poisoned. When she realises they are dying Luisa reveals the truth to Rodolfo, who kills Wurm in revenge.

opera and took steps to enforce the contract. Realising that the composer was beyond their reach they decided to lean on Cammarano, threatening the poor man with imprisonment if he failed to deliver.

With a wife and large family to support he wrote to Verdi begging for help, to which the composer replied that although he was 'able to be scornful of the management's threats' he would compose a new opera for Cammarano's sake 'even if I have to steal two hours every day from my rest, and so from my health!'

Verdi wanted a 'brief drama with plenty of interest, action and above all feeling, which would make it easier to set to music', and suggested a libretto based on the story of Ferrucio ' . . . one of the greatest martyrs to the cause of Italian freedom.' Cammarano sensibly pointed out that such a subject was unlikely to be approved by the censors, given the political climate of the time, and urged that any topic likely to arouse revolutionary sentiments should be avoided. He went on to suggest an idea based on Schiller's prose play *Kabale und Liebe* (Intrigue and Love), mentioned by Verdi on a previous occasion, which had caught the librettist's imagination. In this way *Luisa Miller* came into being, with a plot set in the Tyrol of the 17th century.

The exchange of letters between Verdi and Cammarano while working on *Luisa Miller* shows much give and take in their creative relationship. The composer proposed a number of changes, some of which Cammarano accepted, others he did not. Always he defended his position with good grace, clear argument and artistic integrity. He said to Verdi they 'must work together like brothers, and that if poetry should never be the slave of the music neither should it be its master . . .' That is the voice of a true poet, not a literary hack or brow-beaten librettist.

The overture to *Luisa Miller* stands on its own merits as a piece of orchestral writing worthy of separate performance in today's concert hall. Of the whole work the distinguished Italian scholar Abramo Basevi, also an opera composer and a near-contemporary of Verdi, declared that it represents the turning point in his development as a major force in Italian opera. He claimed that Act III actually ushers in the great middle period of the composer's career, which includes such masterworks as *Rigoletto, Il Trovatore* and *La Traviata*.

Julian Budden acknowledges the importance of *Luisa Miller* and draws our attention to its many strengths, but stands back from Basevi when he says that anyone who hopes to find in the opera a style 'obtrusively different . . . will be disappointed.' Later in the same study he suggests that it is not *Luisa Miller* that we find at the gateway to the middle period but *Stiffelio*, 'a work of scarcely less significance . . . recently unearthed in its original form'. Just how recently may be judged by the fact that the first revival in modern times was at Parma in December 1968. In Great Britain, the first professional performance was given at the Royal Opera House, Covent Garden, on 25 January 1993.

But this is to anticipate events. We need to return to the Italy of 1849, when the forces of reaction were re-grouping and the revolutionary zeal of 1848 was fast evaporating. The King of Piedmont tried to renew the war against Austria but after suffering disastrous defeats at Custozza and Navara, in March 1849, he fled to exile in Portugal. Three months later the newly-created republic in Rome was overthrown by a French army and the Pope was restored to his throne, but not before the rebel leader Garibaldi and his irregular red-shirted bands had captured the hearts of all freedom-loving Italians by their inspired gallantry and daring. Some of the most dramatic scenes in the whole *Risorgimento* were played out in Rome before Garibaldi was forced to lead his men in retreat across Italy. National and republican movements throughout the country collapsed one after another, and in August the last revolutionary government surrendered in Venice.

Verdi watched all these developments with a growing hopelessness. After the fall of Rome he asked his sculptor friend Vincenzo Luccardi, who lived in the city, to send him news urgently:

> For three days I have been waiting impatiently for your letters. You can well imagine how the catastrophe in Rome has weighed heavily in my thoughts, and it was wrong of you not to write to me immediately. Let's not speak of Rome! . . . . what good would it do? Force still rules the world! Justice? . . . what can it do against bayonets? We can only weep at our disgrace and curse those responsible for so much disaster.

After acquiring a taste for country life with Giuseppina at Passy, near Paris, Verdi decided in the summer of 1849 that the time had come to move back to Busseto, not to the Villa Sant'Agata but to the Palazzo Dordoni, another property he had acquired in the district. The long-awaited return of their prodigal son gave rise to a great deal of excitement among the townspeople, especially those mothers with daughters of marriageable age. But they were disappointed and offended when the great man actually took up residence because he refused all their invitations, and saw only members of the Barezzi family and a handful of very close friends. One of these was the Baroness Eroteide Soldati, the wife of a government minister, who had helped Verdi as a young man and had probably been his lover. However, when he called on her he found that her attentions were directed elsewhere, so he brought his visit to a close as soon as he decently could and allowed his own thoughts to return to Giuseppina, who was on her way to join him.

She had broken her journey in Florence to make arrangements for the future welfare of her first-born child Camillo, the only one of her illegitimate children she was prepared to acknowledge. Now eleven years old, he had been brought up by a 'decent' local family, the Zanobinis. Half the costs of his upbringing and his education had been met by his supposed father, Camillo Cirelli, a minor impresario and theatrical agent who was one of Giuseppina's many lovers during the early part of her turbulent career.

A daughter, Sinforosa, had been born on 9 February 1839. Because there was a confusion about dates Giuseppina was not sure whether the father of her child was the impresario Merelli, the tenor Napoleone Moriani, the baritone Raffaele Monti or Camillo Cirelli himself. In the end it was Cirelli who assumed fatherhood before the little girl was adopted.

A second daughter, Adelina, arrived on 4 November 1841. She was put out to foster-parents, but died of dysentery before her first birthday. 'She was given a pauper's funeral while Giuseppina was busy elsewhere,' Gaia Servadio tells us bitterly. It is known that there were other pregnancies which either miscarried or were aborted.

That she did not rear her two surviving children herself, or entrust them to the care of her mother or of her sisters until she was able to look after them, might suggest that Giuseppina Strepponi was a heartless and callous young woman interested only in her career as a singer, and determined to further that career by all possible means. Promiscuous behaviour was socially acceptable, especially in 'artistic' circles, but unwanted pregnancies were not. But are today's standards much different? Hypocrisy changes very little over the years.

When her children were born she had very little money, and to have given up her career to look after them would have risked financial disaster, and ruined any chance of finding a wealthy protector or future husband. Nearly ten years later she was a woman of some substance, having worked hard and successfully in Paris and having managed her financial affairs with considerable prudence and skill. Now she was in a position to show maternal concern, although why that was extended only to her son and not to her daughter is not so easy to understand: perhaps she was anxious not to disturb a successful fosterhood. But she set aside funds for Camillo, and instructed her agent in Florence to take out investments on his behalf.

Having settled these matters she travelled on to the city of Parma where she found Verdi waiting for her in the Hotel Corona. They did a little nostalgic sightseeing before moving on to Borgo San Donnino, where Verdi's new carriage and Emanuele Muzio awaited them. 'Emanuele can come along on foot', said Giuseppina. With Verdi at her side she made her entry into Busseto and saw for the first time the elegant Palazzo Dordoni to which she had been invited – but for how long a stay she still did not know.

Her arrival set tongues a-wagging more furiously than ever. 'How dare Verdi bring *that woman* into his house, to live together quite openly as man and wife?' 'Who does she think she is, with her airs and graces? A singer indeed! – nothing more than a common whore if you ask me.' The good people of Busseto were affronted by her presence, and directed all their insults and abuse at her in a determined effort to drive her away. Within a week or so the town's favourite son became a target: even people close to him expressed their doubts and displeasure.

But inside the Palazzo work went on as if nothing at all were amiss. With Muzio and now Giuseppina at his side Verdi returned to the score of *Luisa Miller*. By October 1849 he was ready to go to Naples to supervise rehearsals and, with his father-in-law as travelling companion, he set off for Rome on the first stage of the journey. On their arrival they found quarantine restrictions in force after an outbreak of cholera in Naples. Unable to go further, at least for the time being, they put their time to good use by visiting Ischia, Herculaneum, Pompeii and other well-known local places of interest. On account of this delay it was agreed to postpone the premiere of the opera until 8 December.

When Verdi finally reached his destination his adventures were by no means at an end, for almost at once he found himself caught up in an ugly and ridiculous dispute with the management of the Teatro San Carlo. He had been advised by Cammarano to insist on being paid for his work before handing it over because the theatre's finances were unsound. The management refused and threatened to have Verdi arrested if he tried to leave the city. Not to be outdone, the composer declared that he would take himself off to a French warship which lay at anchor in Naples harbour, and seek protection until everyone came to their senses. The splendid bluff worked; the management climbed down, and rehearsals for *Luisa Miller* got under way. But Verdi added the Teatro San Carlo to the list of houses he vowed never to work with again.

He left after conducting three performances, all of which were well received by the local audiences. Barezzi had already returned home after attending a few of the early rehearsals. Verdi now followed by sea to Genoa and then by road to Busseto, where Giuseppina was waiting for him.

Well before the row in Naples he had promised Flauto another opera for the early part of the 1850 season, but since this was now ruled out he turned to Cammarano once more and sought his collaboration in a new piece for Ricordi. Once again *King Lear* came into view. In February 1850 Verdi produced a prose version of the play for Cammarano to go through in some detail, but nothing more happened. By April he had taken on a further commitment by signing a contract for a new opera at La Fenice. Now two works had to be written at short notice, and once again Piave was called in to help. His reputation was growing, and while we cannot be certain that Verdi treated him with more respect, he does appear to have given more weight to the librettist's ideas and suggestions than he had done in the past.

Among the various proposals they considered was a work based on Victor Hugo's play *Le Roi s'amuse*, which Verdi had already mentioned to Flauto in September 1849, and another play suggested by Piave with the rather cumbersome title *Le Pasteur, ou L'Evangile et le Foyer*, written by Emile Souvestra and Eugéne Bourgeois. It was an astonishing choice for Verdi to have agreed, partly because the theme of *Stiffelio*, as it became

One of the first perfor-
mances in modern times
of *Aroldo* – Verdi's
unsuccessful re-working
of his earlier opera
Stiffelio – was given by
the State Opera of
Hamburg in 1954.

known, is quite different from any of his previous operas, and partly because it is a realistic drama in a bourgeois setting involving people who, if not ordinary in the usual sense of the word, are certainly not heroic or larger than life. Even more than *Luisa Miller* it is a foretaste of the *verismo* (realism) style of opera which was to become popular later in the 19th century.

Ricordi ran into deep trouble with the censors when he came to present the piece. Several damaging cuts had to be made before the first night, and the new work had a very mixed reception from the critics. One who stood out from the crowd was Francesco Hermet: writing in *La Favilla* he understood what the censors had done and ridiculed them, describing Verdi's music as 'sublime and philosophical'. Other critics shared the confusion of the audience and their inability to grasp the plot. As the veteran English conductor and Verdi specialist Sir Charles Groves has pointed out:

> The Italians thought that if a married man found out that his wife had committed adultery, he wouldn't forgive her – he'd knife her.

A greatly altered version, *Guglielmo Wellingrode*, fared no better when it was staged in Florence a year later, and by 1854 Verdi was convinced that the opera had no future. He took the original autograph, throwing away certain sections and adding new material. But unlike most of his re-workings the new version, entitled *Aroldo* and first performed in Rimini on 16 August 1867, was inferior to the original. For many years it was assumed that *Stiffelio* had been totally lost, and it was not until forgotten manuscripts were discovered in the archives of the Teatro San Carlo that it proved possible for musicologists to reconstruct the opera as it was first written.

When the first professional production in Great Britain was mounted at Covent Garden in January 1993, *Times* critic Rodney Milnes described *Stiffelio* as:

an astonishing opera, unlike anything else in the canon – *Traviata* is the nearest – and pole-axing in its feeling and dramatic impact . . . [It is] a score of bewildering richness, suffused with love and compassion for the erring wife.

The recent restoration of so important an opera has not only enriched the Verdian repertoire of our time, but has also added to our understanding of the way in which Verdi's creative genius continued to develop during the approach to the three great middle-period operas *Rigoletto*, *Il Trovatore* and *La Traviata*.

Chapter 7

The Jester and the Gypsy

In November 1832 Victor Hugo's play *Le Roi s'amuse* was banned the day after it was first performed at the Théâtre Français in Paris, and was not seen again until 50 years later. The author was, however, allowed to publish the text. In a preface stoutly defending his work he summarised the plot and described the principal character, Triboulet:

> . . . deformed . . . sick . . . a court jester – a triple misfortune which makes him evil. Triboulet hates the king because he is a king, the nobles because they are nobles, his fellow-men because they have no humps on their backs . . . The king he depraves, corrupts and brutalizes; he urges him on to tyranny, to vice and ignorance: he unleashes him against all the high-born families, continually pointing out to him the wife to seduce, the sister to carry off, the daughter to dishonour . .
>
> Triboulet has two pupils, the king whom he instructs in vice, the daughter whom he rears in virtue. One will destroy the other. He wants to carry off Madame de Cossé for the king, but it is his own daughter whom he helps to carry off. He wants to murder the king to avenge his daughter, and it is his daughter whom he murders. The punishment does not stop half-way. The curse of Diane's father will be fulfilled on the father of Blanche.

Towards the end of April 1850 Verdi wrote to Piave with an enthusiasm that suggests that he had only recently come across Hugo's play. In fact, it had been in his mind for nearly six years:

> *Le Roi s'amuse* is the greatest subject and perhaps the greatest drama of modern times. Triboulet is a subject worthy of Shakespeare! Just like *Ernani* it's a subject that can't fail . . . Now, going over the various subjects in my mind *Le Roi* came on me like a flash of lightning, and inspiration, and I said to myself . . . 'Yes, by God, that one can't go wrong.'

Having made up his mind to go ahead, Verdi wanted everything done in a hurry. He knew that the plot would attract the unwelcome attention of the censors, and sent Piave off 'to find someone of influence to get us permission to do *Le Roi s'amuse*. Don't go to sleep; give yourself a good shake; do it at once. I shall expect you at Busseto, but not now, after they've agreed the subject.'

It seems that Piave obtained some kind of assurance that objections

Tito Gobbi as Rigoletto
with Renato Scotto as
his daughter, Gilda, in
the BBC1 television
series *Great Characters
in Opera*.

would not be raised, but the details are far from clear. What is known is that by August, Marzari, the director of the Teatro La Fenice, had voiced misgivings about *La maledizione* (The Curse), as the project was now known. There came a characteristic response:

> The doubt you express . . . puts me in a very embarrassing position. I was assured by Piave that there would be no difficulty about this subject and I, trusting his word, set myself to study it and ponder deeply on it and . . . the main part of the work has already been done. If I were now obliged to apply myself to another subject I wouldn't have enough time at my disposal . . . and I couldn't write an opera which would satisfy my artistic conscience . . .

This was special pleading on Verdi's part because he did not receive Piave's complete draft until October. Marzari asked for a copy so that it could be sent to the censors, who were fully aware that the original play had been banned for its 'abundant immorality'. The portrayal of a monarch as a heartless libertine together with an abduction scene and an attempted regicide could have done little to reassure them, but they nevertheless expressed the hope that '. . . the plot would be treated in a fitting manner.'

Worse was to follow, for in December a total ban on the work was imposed by the Military Governor in Venice, who expressed his regret that 'the poet Piave and the celebrated maestro have not chosen some other field to display their talents than the revolting immorality and obscene triviality of the libretto *La maledizione*, submitted to us for eventual performance at La Fenice.'

In an attempt to deal with a deteriorating situation, and although 'no further inquiries in this matter' were to be made, various changes to the plot of *La maledizione* were suggested, none of which the composer found acceptable. One of the many objections was that the principal character was a hunchback. 'Why not?' demanded Verdi. 'I thought it would be beautiful to portray this exceedingly deformed and ridiculous character who is inwardly passionate and full of love.' He went on to repeat his threat that if the qualities of the text were destroyed by cuts he would 'no longer be able to set it to music.'

Finally, at Marzari's suggestion, an urgent meeting was arranged at Busseto to discuss matters. It was agreed, among other things, to change the venue from the court of France to a duchy, either in France or in Italy, and to change the names of the characters. In this way the King (originally François I) became the Duke of Mantua, Triboulet became Rigoletto, whose name was now to be used for the title of the opera, his daughter Blanche became Gilda, and so on. It was also agreed that because of the delays the opening night would have to be postponed until February or March of the following year. These proposals were put to the authorities and after much patient and skilful negotiation a triumphant Piave declared, on 26 January 1851, that *Rigoletto* had arrived 'safe and sound without fractures or amputations.'

Rigoletto contains arias and a quartet familiar to people who have never in their lives set foot in an opera house or watched a full-length opera on television. Probably the most famous is the Duke's song early in Act III, *La donna è mobile*, in which, with mocking humour, he complains

16th century Mantua. The licentious Duke of Mantua has seduced the daughter of Count Monterone who lays a curse on him, and on his mocking hunchbacked court jester Rigoletto. The courtiers, who distrust and hate Rigoletto, discover he has a young girl hidden away, unaware that she is his beautiful daughter, Gilda, carefully guarded from the world. The Duke has already noticed her and disguised as a student declares his love, to which she innocently responds. The courtiers conspire to abduct her and with Rigoletto's unwitting assistance they carry her off to the Duke's bedchamber. When Rigoletto discovers the truth he swears revenge and hires Sparafucile, an assassin, who lures the Duke to an isolated inn where his sister and accomplice, Maddalena, lies in wait.

Rigoletto and his daughter hide in the darkness outside. As Maddalena is serenaded Gilda tells her father that she still loves the Duke despite everything that has happened. Rigoletto sends her home to prepare for their flight from Mantua, but after donning a man's cloak she returns secretly to the scene. Meanwhile, charmed by the Duke, Maddalena persuades her brother not to murder him, but to kill in his place the next visitor to arrive at the inn. Their plan is overheard by Gilda, who decides to sacrifice herself. A fierce storm suddenly blows up; Gilda flings open the door of the inn; Sparafucile stabs her and wraps her body in a sack. A gloating Rigoletto arrives to collect the sack but as he carries it away he is horrified to hear the Duke's voice. He unties the sack to reveal his dying daughter, and collapses in anguish as he realises that Count Monterone's curse has been fulfilled.

about the infidelity of women. Verdi knew he had a tune errand boys would be whistling and that within hours of the first rehearsal it would be ground out by innumerable hurdy-gurdies in the streets. Impact on the opening night would be completely lost and he would suffer, as he had in the past, from unauthorised versions of a popular tune being leaked in advance.

There was little that could be done about plagiarism, but Verdi was determined to protect his reputation and his rights as far as possible. So he withheld the tenor's copy of this *canzone,* together with all the orchestral parts, until the eve of the first performance. Not until the last possible moment did Verdi hand out the parts, and as he did so he swore the tenor, Raffaele Mirate, the orchestra and even the theatre staff, to total secrecy. The simplicity of the scoring made this subterfuge possible; the secret was well kept, and the effect of the song was 'prodigious', as Arthur Pougin tells us in *Verdi, an Anecdotic History of His Life and Works,* published in 1887:

Even from the elegant opening passage of the violins the public was aroused by the freedom and form of the subject; and when the tenor had finished the first verse, thunders of applause broke out in the house, followed after the second by a formidable encore. It was a perfect triumph, as spontaneous as possible.

The character of the Duke of Mantua is immediately established in the opening scene, set in a great hall of the palace with much feasting and revelry. In the sprightly *Questa o quella* (literally, 'this one or that one') his cavalier attitude to women is set out clearly enough. *La donna è mobile* comes later in the opera; some critics say that the tune is too unsophisticated for an aristocrat and highly intelligent Duke. Julian Budden describes it as ' . . . a frankly popular not to say plebeian melody . . . Its very catchiness, so essential to the drama, has in the past given the opera a bad name.' What cannot be denied, however, is that the tune, whatever its merits or faults, serves a dramatic purpose, for its brilliance contrasts powerfully with the gloomy setting of Sparafucile's inn with all its sinister foreboding.

No less famous is the quartet *Bella figlia dell'amore* that follows: ('beautiful daughter of love' hardly conveys the flavour of the original Italian), in which the Duke sings to the seductive Maddalena while, outside the inn, Gilda and Rigoletto add their own observations on what has happened so far. The way in which Verdi has the four characters expressing their different emotions and reactions at the same time is a miraculous piece of writing for the voice. Victor Hugo, who was jealous of Verdi's success and managed to prevent the opera being performed in Paris for at least six years, came to acknowledge its greatness and somewhat ruefully admitted that:

> If only I could make four characters in my play speak simultaneously, and have the audience grasp the words and the sentiments, I would obtain the very same effect.

It used to be thought that this very Mozartian operatic device came to Verdi suddenly in mid-career, but we can now see that he was reaching forward towards it in *Stiffelio* and other pre-*Rigoletto* operas.

Gilda's most famous and, indeed, her only aria *Caro nome* (Beloved name) comes towards the end of Act I after she has been expertly courted by 'Gualtier Maldé', the Duke of Mantua disguised as a student. First heard in the woodwinds, there is a child-like quality in the melody with its repeated cadences that tenderly conveys Gilda's vulnerability and her innocence. It has become a concert platform favourite, of course, and has suffered as a result. If only singers would remember that it is a very simple melody, and if only they could be persuaded to observe Verdi's markings, most performances would be more convincing than in fact they are. As it is, too many sopranos, their own virginity doubtless a fading memory, manage only to be more coy than innocent; more arch than vulnerable.

Rigoletto's malevolent presence can be seen, felt and heard from the outset, as he bursts on to the stage with a great humourless laugh and proceeds to taunt one of the courtiers about his supposedly unfaithful wife: *In testa che avete, Signor di Ceprano?* (What have you got on your head, my Lord Ceprano?). As court jester he carries a 'folly', a *papier maché* puppet grotesquely representing his own features, mounted on a stick and decorated with ribbons and miniature bells, to whom he often addresses his asides and confidences. One of the leading interpreters in recent years was the Italian baritone Tito Gobbi, who had this to say about his role:

> True, his faults are easy to number, but his power to love is as great as the agonies which punctuate his pitiless destiny . . . Rigoletto is a desperate man and desperately defends his job, however ignoble and dangerously offensive he may be. He relies on the protection of his

master and, in any case, this job of his is the only means he has of keeping his daughter in comfort and safely cared for. She is the only creature in the world who matters to him, and for her he destroys himself.

In the final scene of the opera where Rigoletto cradles Gilda in his arms and then, as she dies, utters the terrible cry *Ah, la maledizione*, Gobbi had the jester drop lifeless over his daughter's body as the curtain fell. There is nothing in the libretto or the stage directions to support this *coup de théâtre* but, as Gobbi explains:

Verdi has imagined, described and sung everything. It is for the singer only to shed the light of devoted interpretation upon those treasures entrusted to him . . . It is not written that Rigoletto dies, but I have always thought that the last thing one could wish the poor jester is that he should live to tear his hair fruitlessly. Better death – and our compassion.

The triumph of *Rigoletto* rests upon Verdi's growing powers of characterization, his increasingly subtle and effective use of the orchestra and, most importantly, upon the opera's originality of form. His predecessors, Rossini, Bellini, Donizetti, Mercadante and many others, had followed the classical tradition by hanging their musical material in an orderly, almost predictable, sequence on a framework which would have been familiar to their audiences.

Choruses, arias with half-spoken, half-sung introductions, known as 'dry' recitative when accompanied by a single instrument, usually keyboard, and *accompagnato* with orchestra; other solo items such as serenades and *canzonas* that do nothing to advance the action, but help the development of character and give performers attractive numbers to sing (Mozart's *Voi che sapete* in *The Marriage of Figaro* is a typical example); together with duets, trios, quartets and more intricate ensembles, according to the nature of the drama and the number of characters involved. Towards the end of each of these items there would usually be a *stretto* (literally; narrow) passage in which the pace of the music increased to build up tension and to produce a climax of excitement leading to a rousing finale.

Verdi himself, of course, had followed these conventions, but in *Rigoletto* he sweeps them away to create a free and unified structure in which the music follows and responds to the drama, but is not subordinate to it or shackled to any rigid pattern or formula. His idea was that the opera should consist of 'a long series of duets, without arias and without finales.' The result, paradoxically perhaps, is a greater continuity and cohesion in the music, as well as in the unfolding of the drama, than in anything he had written hitherto.

There were, as we have seen, earlier hints of this new freedom at work. In a letter to Felice Varesi, the celebrated baritone who created the role of Macbeth, Verdi said:

I shall never stop telling you to study the words and the dramatic situation, then the music will come right of its own accord.

However, it is *Rigoletto* that really breaks the mould and clears the way for the future. When the final curtain fell on the night of 11 March 1851 in the Teatro La Fenice in Venice, it came down not only on the first performance of Verdi's new opera, but also on the whole of the early Romantic tradition. On that night, modern Italian opera was born.

Unlike many composers Verdi managed his financial affairs with such skill that even before the success of *Rigoletto* he could, like Rossini, have given up writing music altogether and have lived comfortably on the income generated by the operas he had written up to 1850. From time to time he would tease his Milanese hostesses that this was what he actually planned to do. After his early lessons from Giuseppina Strepponi he required no further instruction regarding the intricacies of the opera business. Letters in the *Copialettere* bear witness to the fact that he drove hard bargains with opera house managers and publishers, and took pains to ensure that the various conditions in his contracts were followed to the letter. It is true that he virtually priced himself out of the market on more than one occasion, but Verdi generally steered a shrewd and prudent course to earn as much as he could from his labours. And who could blame him, especially at a time when copyrights were not protected and pirate productions were the order of the day.

As early as 1845 he had made enough money to buy his *palazzo* in the centre of Busseto: to the townspeople there could not have been a clearer statement of his long-term intentions. By May 1851 the farmhouse at Sant'Agata was ready for occupation, where he and Giuseppina were to live in rural solitude for the rest of their lives. Carlo Verdi had by this time proved an inefficient custodian of his son's property: Verdi not only had to bale him out, but was also reduced to communicating with him, on business matters at least, through his lawyer. To add to the unhappiness, Verdi's mother died in June of that year.

The composer exchanged letters with Cammarano about their next venture but there were few signs of the old urgency. The prison years were quietly coming to an end, although Verdi was often reluctant to acknowledge the fact, for between assignments he now had more time to develop his ideas and material free from nagging financial pressures. In the winter of 1851 he and Giuseppina returned to Paris, among other things to discuss with the Paris Opéra a possible new production. In due course, and after many changes of direction, this became *Les Vêpres siciliennes*.

While they were away in France Verdi received a letter from Antonio Barezzi which caused him much distress. The original has been lost for reasons we do not know, but we can gather its general drift from Verdi's reply, of which a few extracts are quoted below:

Paris: 21 January 1852
My dearest father-in-law,

After so long an interval I hardly expected to receive so cold a letter from you, containing, unless I misread them, some remarks that I deeply resent. Were this letter not signed *Antonio Barezzi*, that is by my benefactor, I should reply with great vigour or not at all. As, however, it bears a name I greatly respect, I shall try to persuade you that your rebukes are undeserved . . .

I do not believe that you would have written of your own accord a letter that was bound to distress me, but you live in a place where people take a wicked pleasure in meddling in the affairs of others and disapprove of everything that does not conform to their own ideas. I never mix myself up with other people's business, unless I am asked, and I therefore object to others meddling with mine . . .

What harm is there in my living in retirement, in my preferring not to pay visits to anyone who happens to have a title, in my taking no part in the festivities or rejoicings of other people? If I choose to manage my property because it amuses me and gives me an occupation, what harm, I repeat, is there in that? And who is a penny the worse for it? . . .

I have nothing to hide. In my house there lives a lady, free and independent, and possessed of a fortune that places her beyond the reach of need. Neither I nor she need render account of our actions to any man. Nor does anyone know what our relations are to one another, how we manage our affairs, what bonds exist between us, or whether I have any legal claims upon her or she upon me. Who can say whether she is my wife or not, and, if she is, what private motives may lead us to avoid publishing the fact? Who knows whether that is a good or a bad thing? . . . I trust that you, in all fairness and of your goodness of heart, will not listen to or be influenced by the gossip of a town that – I must say it! – once thought me unworthy to be its organist, and now whispers about my doings and behaviour. I will not put up with it, and I am not the man to shirk a decision, if it becomes necessary. The world is wide, and the loss of twenty or thirty thousand francs will not prevent my finding a home elsewhere. There should be nothing in this letter to offend you, but should anything I have written displease, I beg you to believe upon my honour that this is not my intention. I have always thought of you, and still think of you with pride and gratitude as my benefactor. Farewell, farewell, in our customary friendship . . .

A previous biographer, Ferrucio Bonavia, suggests that there is 'something ludicrous in the lion of Paris becoming the pariah of Busseto.'

IL TROVATORE
Teatro Apollo, Rome
19 January 1853

In 15th century Spain a gypsy woman, Azucena, seeks revenge for the death of her mother who, some years earlier, was wrongly accused of witchcraft and burned at the stake on the orders of the Count di Luna. Azucena seized one of his two infant sons intending to inflict a similar death upon him, but in her frenzy she threw her own son into the fire by mistake. She has reared the Count's child, Manrico, as her own: only she knows his true identity. On reaching manhood he becomes a troubadour and leader of a rebel band. Meanwhile his brother has succeeded to the title and has become the commander of the Prince of Aragon's army. Both he and Manrico love Leonora, lady-in-waiting to the Princess of Aragon.

Azucena falls into the hands of the young Count di Luna's forces and is recognised as the supposed killer of his brother. Manrico tries to rescue her but is captured in the attempt. To gain his freedom Leonora offers herself to di Luna: he accepts her proposal, whereupon she takes a slow-acting poison. Furious at being duped, di Luna refuses to release Manrico but has him executed instead. An exultant Azucena reveals that he has just killed his own brother: her mother's death has at long last been avenged.

Soon after the first performance in England of *Il Trovatore*, at the Drury Lane Theatre in 1856, song sheets began to appear. This typical illustration shows Manrico and Azucena as prisoners of the Count di Luna.

Yet the hostility in the town was real enough. What might strike the Anglo-Saxon reader as odd is the equivocal nature of Verdi's reply in what was, by his own admission, a 'long and rambling letter'. Is he not being rather less than honest when he asks '. . . who can say whether she is my wife or not?' Is this an honourable way to treat a father-in-law he respects, especially when there is no suggestion that Barezzi has in any way changed his own high opinion of Giuseppina? It is difficult to escape the conclusion that Verdi is, once again, adjusting the libretto.

When Cammarano failed to respond to the *King Lear* proposal, Verdi seems to have accepted the situation with good grace and suggested, as an alternative, an opera based on *El Trovador*, a play by the Spanish dramatist García Gutiérrez, first performed in Madrid in August 1836. How Verdi came across this work is a mystery because no translation existed at the time. It was left to Giuseppina to prepare an Italian version; Cammarano was assured that it was 'very beautiful, imaginative and full of strong situations'. However, by March 1851 Verdi had heard nothing from him, and was losing patience. 'Does he like it or doesn't he?' was the question he put to their mutual friend De Sanctis: 'do beg him not to lose a moment more time.' When Cammarano did reply, he had so many reservations that Verdi asked in some exasperation, 'If you didn't share my opinion, why didn't you suggest another plot?'

Verdi left Cammarano in no doubt that he had been attracted to *Il Trovatore* because it seemed to offer 'excellent dramatic features and, in addition, something singular and original.' The romantic melodrama, and the powerful central character of Azucena, met his need exactly for the 'boldest possible subjects, clad in the newest forms'. The lack of an enthusiastic response from his librettist was disappointing: on 9 April 1851 he wrote once more:

> I have read your scenario, and, being a man of talent and superior character, you will hardly be offended if I tell you that if this subject, on our stage, cannot incorporate all the freshness and strangeness of the Spanish play, it would be better to give it up . . . Azucena particularly lacks her essential strangeness and novelty of character . . . we preserve to the very last this woman's two great passions: her love for Manrico and her burning thirst to avenge her mother's death.

Verdi understood more clearly than his librettists that most of his operas were driven by that most powerful of all motives, the lust for vengeance, *la vendetta*, and that this more than anything else accounted for their dramatic force.

It has been suggested by Feruccio Bonavia, among others, that Verdi failed to realize the 'confusion that must inevitably ensue when many incidents, first reduced to the bare bones and then magnified by music, follow in rapid succession and from one place to another.' But such criticism, itself, fails to take into account Verdi's formidable stage-craft, his great skill in arranging and presenting his material, and his firm grasp of structure and form.

Nowhere are these qualities more clearly demonstrated than in the opening scenes of the opera where, after a brief and highly-charged introduction to establish the prevailing mood of the drama, three long narrative passages give the background to the action. These passages are scored in a deceptively simple manner. A close analysis of the music, beyond my present scope, reveals much inspired detail in the way the melodies are structured, in Verdi's harmonic textures and his use of contrasting and matching keys.

First we learn of the 'gypsy hag' burned at the stake for witchcraft, Azucena's seizure of the infant son of Count di Luna and the grisly discovery of 'a child's bones, half-burned and still smouldering.' Next, Leonora confesses her love for Manrico with the prophetic words 'Either I shall live for him, or I shall die!': the young Count di Luna overhears her and the fierce jealousy between the two men is clearly revealed. Then, in the opening scene of Act II, after the 'Anvil Chorus', Azucena tells Manrico about her mother's death, her quest for vengeance and how in her anguish she committed the wrong child to the flames.

Only at this point is the stage set and the audience fully prepared for the unfolding of the double drama that follows – the rivalry between Manrico and the Count over Leonora, and the conflict in the heart of Azucena. Whatever might be said about the extravagant and improbable nature of the plot, with all its grotesque horror, Verdi sets out his complex argument logically and with economy of means. Not a word is wasted; not a note is out of place.

Cammarano set to one side his earlier misgivings and accepted Verdi's treatment without further reservation or qualification. His language was often archaic and fustian, but he always wrote his texts with the composer's needs uppermost in his mind. For him, collaboration between writer and musician was a partnership between creative equals. Verdi understood this very well, and once the broad outlines and the structure of a new work were established he was prepared to leave his librettist to do the rest: '. . . When one has a Cammarano, one can hardly go wrong.'

However, work on the opera made slow progress. On Giuseppina's advice no commitments had been entered into with publishers or with theatre managers, so there were no deadlines to meet. Verdi was now free to follow his own course and to set his own timetable. This was, of course, a welcome and beneficial change, but the lifting of pressure made it more difficult to deal with Cammarano's lack of any sense of urgency.

Verdi's life as a successful composer imposed many other demands. As his reputation continued to grow the number of new productions of his existing operas increased, as did the proposals for new commissions all of which had to be carefully evaluated. The proper management of his financial affairs, including the collection of fees and royalties from an ever-growing number of contracts and rights agreements, not to mention the new burdens of estate management, meant that even with the devoted assistance both of Muzio and of Giuseppina, Verdi now had to devote a great deal of his energy and time to routine matters.

His mother's death in June 1851 had hit him hard; the hostility of his neighbours in Busseto caused him concern for Giuseppina's sake, if not for his own. His father, with whom his relations were still uneasy, was another source of anxiety: he became seriously ill towards the end of the year and remained so for several months. Then in February 1852, when Verdi was in Paris, came unsettling news about Cammarano's health.

Despite these difficulties, by May 1852 Verdi felt able to offer *Il Trovatore* to the Teatro San Carlo for production towards the end of the year. Apparently he had put to one side his vow not to write for them again, but the fee he demanded proved too much for the Naples management who broke off the negotiation. The composer then approached the Rome impresario Vincenzo Jacovacci at the Teatro Apollo, to whom he was under some obligation. Terms were agreed without delay. While these moves were afoot, Verdi wrote once again to Cesare De Sanctis:

> I haven't had any more news of Cammarano, so I think he must be completely recovered. Ask him to send me the remainder of the libretto as soon as possible, and tell him that, when this is finished, if he would like to do another one for me, I should be delighted.

But it was already too late, for by this time Cammarano was dead. Verdi read the news 'not in a letter from a friend, but in a stupid theatrical journal'. Was this a stinging rebuke to De Sanctis for not telling him? In a letter expressing his grief he goes on to say:

> It is impossible to describe my sadness to you. You loved him as much as I did, and will understand the feelings I cannot put into words. Poor Cammarano. What a loss.

Very little work remained to be done on the libretto and De Sanctis suggested that Emmanuele Bardare, a pupil of Cammarano, should be asked to finish it. He also drew attention to the desperate plight of Cammarano's family. In reply Verdi immediately sent six hundred ducats to the widow, one hundred ducats more than the agreed fee. As a further step he renounced, for the time being at least, ownership of his scheme for *King Lear* and of the draft libretto Cammarano had prepared, in the hope that they might yield income for the bereaved family.

By September 1852, with an assurance from De Sanctis that the singers at the Teatro Apollo were up to their task, and with a libretto safely in his hands Verdi was at last ready to put pen to paper. In this respect his composing method ran true to form: usually he refused to write music until he had the words in front of him 'because when I have a general idea of the entire work, the notes come of their own accord.'

But *Il Trovatore* differed from all his previous operas in one important respect: he had lived with it for nearly three years – a period of gestation totally without precedent.

Whether, like Beethoven, he was to able to carry his musical ideas with him a long time ('long', in Verdi's case, being a relative term), or whether there was a great release of creative energy when he returned to his piano and to his writing desk it is impossible to say. But the music he composed for *Il Trovatore* has a forward momentum that carries us through the complex absurdities of the plot, and holds us spellbound to the end.

Although there is only one real character in the opera – the gypsy heroine Acuzena, who attracted Verdi to his subject in the first place – we accept the remaining cut-out cardboard figures on the stage because the music is so powerful. And we overlook, too, the return to those out-dated operatic forms dictated by high melodrama to which Cammarano was so firmly attached. The music is of such intensity and such lyricism, and is so full of melodic invention, that none of this really matters. Verdi may have sounded the death-knell of the old bel canto traditions in *Rigoletto*, but in *Il Trovatore* he accorded them a fitting and impassioned Requiem.

The night before a triumphant first performance on 19 January 1853 the river Tiber burst its banks and flooded the low-lying area of Rome where the Teatro Apollo stood. 'Perhaps a symbol,' the Italian scholar Marcello Conati suggests, 'of the deluge caused by the opera as it flooded European stages with its melodies, and swept, after only a few years, over the remotest corners of the five continents.'

That triumph in Rome was followed by thirty different productions in Italy, Malta and Corfu during the first year. In 1853 the figure more than doubled, and well before the end of the decade *Il Trovatore* had been seen all over Europe, as well as in South America and the Middle East. The opera was not, and is not, without its critics: it is easy to be outraged by the grotesque plot and the commonplace vulgarities in the music. But ordinary opera lovers the world over discovered immediately what took many experts so long to recognise: *Il Trovatore* is one of the most remarkable and most memorable of all Verdi's operas.

Chapter 8

Who was
La Traviata?

One evening in February 1852 Verdi and Giuseppina went to the Vaudeville Theatre in Paris to see *La dame aux camélias* by Alexandre Dumas. A dramatisation of his earlier novel of the same name, the play draws its inspiration partly from Abbé Prévost's *Manon Lescaut*, and partly from the young writer's own experience. It is the classic story of a beautiful courtesan who falls in love with a young man of slender means, unable to sustain her luxurious way of life. Dumas, who was known as Dumas *fils to* distinguish him from his famous father, made no secret of the fact that his book was based on his own passionate love affair with Marie Alphonsine Duplessis, one of the most celebrated and sought-after Parisian *demi-mondaines*, who was loved and admired by artists as well as by many rich and famous men. He describes her in this way:

> . . . tall, very thin, dark-haired and with a pink-and-white complexion. Her head was small, her eyes long and slanting like those of a Japanese woman but lively and alert. Her lips were the colour of cherries and she had the most beautiful teeth in the world. She was like a Saxe figurine.

While Dumas was in her Paris apartment with a group of friends Marie was suddenly seized by a fit of coughing and withdrew to her bedroom. Dumas followed and was horrified to find her coughing blood. She was so overcome by his genuine anxiety and tender care that shortly afterwards they became lovers, but it was a doomed affair. She did, indeed, love the young writer, but the thought of giving up her life of luxury and all her other lovers probably never entered her mind. Had it done so she would have dismissed it at once, in true Gallic style, with a single shake of her pretty head.

Marie eventually married a Vicomte de Pérrigaux at the Kensington Registry Office in London, but shortly afterwards she deserted him as well. On her return to France she visited a number of spas in an attempt to find a cure for her disease, but to no avail. She died in Paris in 1847, at the age of twenty-three, and was given a spectacular funeral before being laid to rest in a Montmartre cemetery.

In the hands of Alexandre Dumas the real Marie Duplessis became the fictional Marguerite Gautier: in Verdi's hands she became Violetta. 'When Giuseppina read the novel and then saw the play together with Verdi, she must have been struck with a curious sensation of *déjà vu,*' says Gaia

Servadio. Writing 'as a woman of the twentieth century', she believes that 'Giuseppina was led astray – *traviata* – by her own century in more ways than one.'

The emphasis on the word *traviata* is significant because the usual translation 'The Fallen Woman' does not capture in English its full, elusive meaning. The 'fragile' or the 'weak woman' is nearer the mark: one who is not only easily led astray, not only weak in a physical sense, which might also encompass ill-health and disability, but also one who is extremely vulnerable in a male-dominated society.

Of the fact that Strepponi did not die of a mortal illness as a young woman but lived on to venerable old age, Gaia Servadio has this to say:

> In one sense, this Giuseppina-Violetta, who made a name for herself in the musical world, who struggled to maintain a position of her own, does die because she gives up the stage to become a different woman, Signora Verdi . . .

The parallel between Giuseppina's earlier intemperate style of living and the careers of the tragic heroines is obvious. So, too, is the point that the glamorous, shadowy world of actresses and singers was not far removed from that of the *demi-mondaines*. However, further speculation on these lines is not encouraged by Julian Budden:

> . . . the notion that Verdi, while insisting on the respect due to the woman who now shared his life, should then have insulted her himself by portraying her as a *demi-mondaine* is surely preposterous. One can imagine his blind fury if the idea were put to him.

This is a powerful argument, and the absence of written evidence pointing to any link in Verdi's mind between Violetta and Giuseppina seems quite conclusive. Yet does not the shadow of a doubt remain? The fires of creation burn in mysterious and unexpected ways: who is to say what really went on at subconscious level as Verdi's genius flared, and as his ideas danced and sparkled in the flame?

It was during his stay in Paris early in 1852 that the Venetian impresario, Marzari, asked him to write a new opera for the La Fenice carnival season in March the following year. It seems unlikely that Verdi had the Dumas play in mind as a possible subject at so early a stage as he insisted on a *donna di prima forza* for one of the principal roles – hardly a fitting description for a singer intended to play the part of a heroine in the final stages of consumption.

The contract was signed in May, when it was agreed that Piave should write the libretto on a subject to be chosen. The summer months passed without any firm proposal coming forward, and by the beginning of October the theatre management had become seriously concerned. The police were pressing hard for a decision so that censorship could be set in motion, and less than six months now remained for the production work to be carried out, not to mention the actual writing of the text and the composition of the music. Piave was sent to Sant'Agata, where Verdi and Giuseppina had at last taken up residence, with firm instructions to get some decisions one way or another.

He took with him an almost complete draft based on one of the topics suggested, but on arrival was disconcerted to find that the Maestro was now 'carried away by another idea. I had to throw away everything I had done and start all over again.' Violetta had triumphed: for what possible reason is examined later.

But by this time, of course, preparations for *Il Trovatore* were well under way. Thanks largely to his own irresolution, a failing which he deplored in others, Verdi now found himself with two operas under preparation at the same time. It was a return to the prison years with the difference that he was no longer completely at the behest of other people: he had brought this new situation upon himself. When the time came for him to take an apartment in Rome, leaving an unhappy Giuseppina to hold the fort at Sant'Agata, he insisted on having a piano of good quality installed so that he could carry on composing the new opera whenever he was not at the Teatro Apollo rehearsing *Il Trovatore*.

The provisional title of the new work was *Amore e Morte* (Love and Death), meat which even the lenient Venice censors found a little too strong, so they insisted on a change. Otherwise they raised no objection to the synopsis despite the daring nature of the subject and the portrayal on stage of a distressing terminal illness. Verdi's morale seems to have held up well under pressure for on New Year's Day 1853 he wrote confidently to De Sanctis:

> For Venice I'm doing *La Dame aux camélias* which will probably be called '*La Traviata*'. A subject for our own age. Another composer wouldn't have done it because of the costumes, the period and a thousand other silly scruples. But I'm writing it with the greatest of pleasure.

As the first night drew nearer, other problems arose. Out of the blue the theatre management decided that settings and costumes should not be contemporary, as Verdi had laid down, but that the opera should be set in or around the year 1700. By this arbitrary decision one of the main planks of Verdi's argument, that this was a 'subject for our time', was removed. There were also difficulties over the choice of Fanny Salvini-Donatelli as prima donna. She was an accomplished and successful Verdian soprano but her lack of acting ability and somewhat matronly appearance made her unsuitable for the role of Violetta. Verdi insisted that the part must be played by someone who 'is young, has a graceful figure and who can sing with passion.' But the management maintained that they were under a contractual obligation to the soprano and refused to give way. Verdi then threatened to 'cancel everything'.

This produced an angry response from the theatre, who reminded the composer of his responsibilities and hastily sent Piave and the La Fenice secretary, Guglielmo Brenna, to Sant'Agata to work out a solution. Scarcely a month remained before the opening night and some sort of compromise was reached, although precisely what we do not know. It became clear, however, that for the most part Verdi's objections were overruled and that his gloomy predictions of disaster were firmly based. 'I shall have a complete fiasco,' he wrote to Piave: 'I know, I know, and I shall prove it to you . . .

On the opening night Alfredo was sung by the tenor Ludovico Graziani, who was unwell, and the crucial role of Germont, Alfredo's father, was sung by Felice Varesi, a distinguished baritone approaching the

Teatro La Fenice, Venice
6 March 1853

Paris: c1850. Alfredo Germont, a young man of good breeding but fairly modest means, is present at a sumptuous party given by the beautiful courtesan Violetta Valéry, who is suffering from consumption. He is a secret admirer and, after the other guests have gone, he declares his love and urges her to give up her way of life. She seizes this last opportunity of requited love and sets up house with Alfredo in the country, where her health apparently improves. Their idyll is shattered when Alfredo's father, Giorgio Germont, suddenly arrives and, finding Violetta alone, tells her that her relationship with his son is destroying his family's reputation and has placed his daughter's forthcoming wedding in jeopardy. Because of her love for Alfredo she cannot resist Germont's entreaties, and agrees to give him up.

After returning to her former protector, Baron Douphol, she meets Alfredo by chance. He bitterly reproaches her and, to his father's fury, throws his gambling winnings at her feet, at which point she collapses. A remorseful Germont reveals the true extent of Violetta's sacrifice. Alfredo rushes to her side: she rallies at his renewed declarations of love but, after a passionate and joyful embrace, dies in his arms.

end of his career, who found the part was 'too difficult' and said that it 'lacked potential'. According to some accounts, there was laughter in the audience when Fanny Salvini-Donatelli attempted to play a dying consumptive. Before any reviews appeared in the press Verdi sent brief reports on this first performance to a few friends, including one of recent acquaintance, the conductor Angelo Mariani:

> *La Traviata* has been an utter fiasco, and what is worse, they laughed. Well, what about it? I'm not worried. Either I'm wrong or they are. I personally don't think that last night's verdict will have been the last word.

There is little, if any, disagreement in the many accounts describing how *La Traviata* came into being, but there are certain pieces of evidence that seem to have been largely ignored possibly because they are not there. The first concerns the almost completed libretto Piave took with him to Sant'Agata. We know that it existed but do not know what it was about, which is odd when we remember that Verdi's reputation had now reached a point where papers were guarded and kept for posterity. Like many of their contemporaries both he and Piave were prodigious note-takers and correspondents, and Giuseppina an intelligent and meticulous archivist, so a great deal of documentary evidence exists. But nothing has survived that provides any clue as to the subject originally chosen for Piave to develop as a finished draft.

The second question that springs to mind is simply this: why, with a first night less than six months away and at a time when he was already occupied with another major opera, *Il Trovatore*, did Verdi turn down a libretto which was almost ready for scoring? He may have had no regard for Piave's feelings and may well have brushed aside his difficulties, but he must also have realized that he was adding considerably to his own problems by acting in this way.

The composer in 1853, the year during which *La Traviata* was first performed.

Lastly, who or what so fired his imagination? Piave tells us that on reaching Sant'Agata 'I could see that he was very worked up.' If any

protest was made about having to discard the work he had already done, no mention is made of the fact. So struck was he by Verdi's attitude that he seems to have accepted the situation without demur and to have buckled down to his fresh task without complaint. 'I think Verdi will write a fine opera', he told a friend: not a word of reproach as far as we know, nor any further comment.

We are left with Verdi's sudden and overwhelming enthusiasm for a subject which, hitherto, had been only one among a number of possible choices. As has been seen, autobiographical considerations are not really in the frame: any attempts to forge a direct link between the character of Violetta with that of Giuseppina Strepponi or, for that matter, between the character of Germont and that of Antonio Barezzi, are ill-advised to say the least.

But is it too far-fetched to suggest that Giuseppina, who we know was deeply impressed by *La dame aux camélias* and who recognised in the heroine something of her own early life, may have impressed upon Verdi the dramatic power of the plot, the humanity and richness of the characters and the scope these qualities had to offer in musical terms?

It seems to me possible to take the view that Strepponi was the real *Traviata* not because Violetta was in any way modelled upon her character or her experience – such connections are far too simplistic – but because her sympathy with the heroine and with her situation enabled Strepponi to impress upon Verdi the rich dramatic and musical potential the Dumas play had to offer. We know how closely she worked with him at this time; we know how much he valued her advice; it can hardly be imagined that they did not discuss the new project together. On the contrary, it is highly likely that at some point, possibly in the still watches of the night, she turned to Verdi and said: 'You know, that Dumas story would make a very good opera: you ought to do something about it.' Only, as an Italian lady, she would not have expressed herself quite in those terms.

At least one further mystery remains. That *La Traviata* was not a runaway success is clear, but not all reviews were unfavourable. On the third night Fanny Salvini-Donatelli was applauded after Act I, and there was applause also after the Finale of Act II. It is true that the death of Violetta was received in silence, but there is no suggestion that the audience burst into laughter. The shortcomings of some of the other principal singers on the opening night have already been noted, but why was Verdi so anxious to tell some of his closest friends, before notices had appeared in the press, that the production had been such a disaster? Was it to justify his gloomy predictions? Or was it to spite a theatre management who had thwarted him on a number of important issues, and with whom he had had so many disagreements?

After the 'fiasco', Verdi forbade any further performances of the opera until he could exercise control over the choice of singers. In doing so he suffered a loss of income, as it was not until a year later that a revival was staged at the Teatro Gallo, formerly the Teatro San Benedetto, which was also in Venice. The composer made some improvements to the score but, once again, he had to yield on the question of costume and period. Piave supervised the production and unlimited rehearsal time was allowed by the impresario, Antonio Gallo, whose confidence in the true worth of *La Traviata* could not be shaken. It was a hunch that paid off for the opera

Verdi's study at the Villa Sant'Agata. The portrait of his father-in-law, Antonio Barezzi, faces the composer's writing table.

was an overnight success; its reputation spread like wildfire throughout the rest of Italy and it quickly became one of the most popular works in the entire Verdi canon.

Opera house managers fell over each other in their efforts to negotiate contracts and Verdi soon found himself embroiled with local censors who lacked the tolerance and vision of those in Venice. After the collapse of the independence movements in 1848/9 most authorities, church and state, clamped down and imposed censorship more rigorously than before. The choice of subject matter came under careful scrutiny once again, and any topic likely to encourage libertarian sentiments was banned. According to the censors, political unreliability went hand-in-hand with sexual freedom, a point of view that suited the purposes of the Church well enough. As a result, restrictions were placed upon Italian writers and artists that would not have been out of place in the most repressive households in Victorian England.

Verdi's reputation was such that he was allowed a freedom denied to lesser mortals, but in the 1850s not even his work was immune from petti-fogging interference and regulation. There exists to this day a copy of the libretto of *La Traviata* 'emended' by a canon of Bologna cathedral, who insisted that the famous Act 1 drinking song, *Libiamo ne'lieti calici* (Let's lift our glasses and drink), was 'licentious' and that it must either be cut or completely re-written. Verdi made a bitter comment about 'those holy priests who cannot bear to see represented on the stage what they do every night behind closed doors.'

In a film version of the opera this same drinking song attracted the attention of the authorities in Bombay during the early 1950s, when determined efforts were being made to enforce Prohibition in various parts of India. Before the film was approved for general release every frame that showed a glass being lifted to the lips had to be edited from the print. The effect of such cuts on the sound track is best left to the reader's imagination.

When *La Traviata* was first performed in London in 1856, Violetta was played by the soprano Piccolomini, better known for her good looks and acting prowess than for her musical ability. Verdi's music was described by the critic of *The Athenaeum* as 'trashy', and he went on to say that:

> The young Italian lady cannot do justice to the music, such as it is. Hence it follows that the opera and the lady can only establish themselves in proportion as Londoners rejoice in a prurient story prettily acted.

This line was developed in a notorious review that appeared in *The Spectator* not long afterwards, which received the rare distinction of being reprinted in full by *The Times* on 4 August 1856:

> The highest society in England has thronged the opera house night after night to see a young and very innocent-looking lady impersonate the heroine of an infamous French novel, who varies her prostitution by a frantic passion . . . Verdi's music, which generally descends below his subjects, can in this case claim the ambiguous merit of being quite worthy of the subject . . . We should have thought the production of *La Traviata* an outrage on the ladies of the aristocracy who support the theatre, if they had not by crowding their boxes every night shown that they did not notice the underlying vice of the opera.

This was followed by editorial comment a few days later:

> A public prostitute . . . coughs her way through three acts and finally expires on the stage in a manner which, however true to nature, ought to be revolting to the feelings of spectators . . . Next season we trust to hear no more such abominations.

Stupid censorship and ill-informed criticism left Verdi completely unmoved, but he was more responsive to public opinion than he cared to admit. When the revival of *La Traviata* scored such spectacular success in May 1854 he told De Sanctis that the opera 'is the same, exactly the same as the one performed last year' apart from some transpositions of key and other minor adjustments 'to suit the capacity of the singers'.

> For the rest not a single piece has been altered, not a piece added or taken away, not a musical idea changed. Everything which was there for the Fenice is there for the Teatro Benedetto. Then it was a fiasco; now it has created a furore. Draw your own conclusions!

In fact the differences between the two versions are more important than Verdi made out, as shown by Julian Budden's analysis. But who would deny the composer the well-earned satisfaction of a dig at La Fenice?

La Traviata has remained one of the most popular of all Italian operas – a popularity that has survived the many changes in public taste and attitudes since it first appeared. Early audiences soon took the plot in their stride and treated the opera as a showcase for the reigning prima donnas of the day. Performances were carefully compared and contrasted by groups of admirers some of whom, like the rowdier elements in a modern football crowd, were literally ready to do battle on behalf of their chosen favourites. Lavish productions were the order of the day – a tradition which has not entirely disappeared – and impresarios outbid their rivals in the opulence of the sets, the richness of the costumes and in the value of the jewellery worn on stage.

Towards the turn of the century, while many chocolate box trimmings remained, greater emphasis was placed on the melodramatic nature of the plot. By this time swooning heroines had become a cliché on the stage: producers could no longer rely on the originality of the story nor upon its realistic representation to command the attention of an audience. So singers were required to point up their movements and their gestures in a manner which would strike us today as extravagant and ludicrous.

For many reasons there were radical changes in public taste at the turn of the century, by which time Verdi's reputation was already in decline. Nevertheless, *La Traviata* remained good box office despite the new brutalism in the air and the sweeping aside of many of the old conventions. By the 1930s, according to Edward J. Dent, 'recent productions have made *La Traviata* a chamber opera of singularly touching delicacy.' Such a description would be unthinkable today: it conjures up part of the production and performing tradition far more remote to us than the colourful, full-blooded melodrama of earlier years.

Although we are no longer shocked or even aware of the sexual components of the plot – pornography has come a long way since Verdi's time – we are appalled by the hypocrisy and complacency of many of the male characters; their attitude to women; their arrogance; their casual disregard for the destruction of a young life. These things matter far more to us than the fact that Violetta was a whore.

Most of today's audiences would neither recognise nor accept 'the singularly touching delicacy of a chamber opera' which Dent describes, but are much more likely to agree with Rodney Milnes when he talks of a 'bitterly angry tragedy'. This modern vision is surely closer to the truth and closer to the composer's original intention and character. As we have seen, anger and bitterness were two of the many strands in the complex personality of Giuseppe Verdi.

One further comment: *La Traviata* makes wonderful theatre. In the score we find some of the composer's most eloquent and expressive melodies. We need look no further for any explanation of the fact that it is one of the most successful operas ever written. But that so much of the music was put down on paper alongside *Il Trovatore*, a work of an entirely different but equally powerful nature, remains one of the great mysteries regarding Verdi's contribution to creative human endeavour.

Chapter 9

Death in Palermo and Other Tales

With the successful completion of the romantic trilogy *Rigoletto*, *Il Trovatore* and *La Traviata* not long before his fortieth birthday, there comes a marked change of tempo in Verdi's creative output. From 1839 to 1853 he had written eighteen operas, apart from numerous re-workings and revisions: during the next thirty years he was to write no more than six operas, again disregarding re-workings, and the great Manzoni *Requiem*.

By 1853 his position as the leading composer of Italian opera was unassailable, his international reputation was well established and the foundations of his personal fortune were firmly laid. Financial imperatives had not completely disappeared, however, for the conversion of Sant'Agata from a modest farmhouse into a well-appointed villa was proving expensive, and Verdi's recently-found ambition to be a country landowner, involving as it did the acquisition of neighbouring fields and vineyards, had to be funded from more than profits made on the farm.

Artistically, the challenge of the Paris Opéra remained: no Italian composer could be said to have truly arrived until French audiences had strewn flowers at his feet. The grand opera tradition established by Meyerbeer's *Robert le Diable* in 1831 and later works of a similar nature was now proving difficult for the directors of the Opéra to sustain, but the vocal and instrumental resources in Paris were still far richer than those at the command of La Scala or any other of the major opera houses in Italy. Not surprisingly, Verdi found the potential offered by such resources extremely tempting.

The French were in grandiloquent mood, possibly by way of compensation for the realities of their discreet, bourgeois, post-Napoleonic world. Not for them the subtle interplay of character to be found in *Rigoletto*, for example: French audiences demanded spectacle on a large scale, with plenty of novelty thrown in for good measure. They still expected five acts and a ballet. 'An opera at the Opéra is enough to stun a bull,' complained Verdi. 'Five hours of music? Phew! . . .'

Such demands ran counter to his own views on the importance and value of brevity, but ever a pragmatic man of the theatre he determined to give the French public what it wanted. Verdi had no time for those who believed that audiences were there to be educated: they came to the theatre to be entertained, and it was his job to fill the seats. Furthermore, as a practical musician he was not content to rest upon his laurels. He knew his artistic self well enough to realise that he needed a new challenge and the stimulus of a fresh and broader canvas on which to work. That he could so in Paris without fear of censorship, but within the disciplines demanded by a different tradition – the French tradition, with its own distinctive forms and conventions – he regarded as an important additional bonus.

It was in 1852, at a time when *Il Trovatore* was uppermost in his thoughts, that he resumed negotiations with the management of the Paris Opéra. His terms were tough. The ageing but distinguished Eugène Scribe was to be his librettist; a synopsis was to be submitted by the end of June and a full libretto completed by the end of the year; rehearsals in a theatre to be placed at Verdi's disposal were to start in July 1854 with singers of his choice; forty performances were to be given within ten months of the opening night, and if any provisions in the contract were breached a sum of 30,000 francs would be payable to him.

After the contract was signed there followed the usual exchange of ideas on the choice of subject. The correspondence with Scribe was desultory and inconclusive, but this did not bother Verdi in the early stages for he had already more than enough on his plate. But when nothing had been agreed by July 1853 he decided to go to Paris in the autumn to force some decisions one way or another.

Much to her delight he took Giuseppina with him, for it soon became clear that if the new grand opera were to be ready on time a great deal of close supervision would be needed and that this would require a long stay in Paris. After being shut away in Busseto for so long, by herself for much of the time and in failing health, Giuseppina relished the prospect of living once again in her favourite city where she would be able to take her place in fashionable and intelligent society, enjoy the elegant shops, and be safely at Verdi's side, away from the envy and malice of spiteful, narrow-minded neighbours.

When they reached Paris they found many changes. After a successful plebiscite followed by a *coup d'état*, Louis Napoleon had himself proclaimed Emperor Napoleon III. One of the first things he did was to instruct Haussmann, who was an architect and Prefect of Police, to clear away the slums of central Paris and to drive open boulevards through the city. His motives were not aesthetic, nor his intentions philanthropic. He fully understood that those who had swept him into power might turn against him at any time. He also realised that wide roads made it easier to control hostile crowds and more difficult to erect barricades. During civil unrest the military could move more freely from place to place and, if necessary, artillery pieces could be more readily be deployed.

The systematic clearance of old houses caused a great deal of hardship among *Les Misérables*, as we know from Victor Hugo's great classic. Verdi himself was greatly intrigued by all the activity going on around him and stopped to watch the workmen whenever he could. Charles Osborne tells us that 'he went out to the Bois de Boulogne to inspect the artificial lakes, and enjoyed watching the destruction of slums between the Louvre and the Tuileries.'

However, he had more pressing matters on hand. Scribe, who had a workshop of younger writers working for him, had so far submitted only a few ideas in a rather half-hearted manner, none of which the composer had found suitable. With Verdi on his doorstep he turned in some desperation to *Le Duc d'Alba*, a libretto he had written fifteen years earlier for Fromental Halévy, a French-Jewish composer of the Meyerbeer school, who eventually rejected it. Scribe then offered his work to Donizetti who kept it for some time but failed to complete a musical score. With difficulty the libretto was recovered from the composer's effects, since when it had 'long been asleep in the dust of the shelves,' as Scribe explained to his collaborator Charles Duveyrier.

The original plot, set in the Netherlands during the 16th century at a time of highly repressive Spanish rule, concerns the Duke of Alba and his illegitimate son, Henri, who foiled an attempt on his father's life at the cost of his own. Verdi wanted to change the setting to Naples, but accepted Scribe's suggestion that Sicily should be chosen instead. From that point on other changes followed logically: the Duke of Alba became the French governor Guy de Montfort and the date was put back to 1282, when the Sicilians actually did rise up in revolt. Historical reality was enriched by grafting on the legend of a massacre at Vespers, to produce the plot of *Les Vêpres siciliennes* as we know it today.

The completed libretto reached Verdi on the last day of 1853, and he started working on it 'very slowly', as he told the Countess Appiani. 'In fact you could even say that I am not writing at all. I don't know how it happens but the libretto is always there in the same place.' The weeks passed and in May came the welcome news of the success of *La Traviata* on its re-launch, as we would now say, in Venice. Not long afterwards the summer heat in Paris became oppressive, and Verdi and Giuseppina escaped to the village of Mandres, between Chaumont and Dijon in the Haute-Marne, where they had rented a house. Here he worked steadily on the new score for three months: by September he was able to report to De Sanctis that four of the five acts were ready.

In October he returned to Paris to start rehearsals only to find, soon after his arrival, that the eccentric German soprano Sofia Cruvelli (Sophie Crüwel) who had been chosen to play the leading part of Hélène, had left Paris without warning and had completely vanished. Messengers were sent out in all directions to find her, but without success. Her sudden disappearance created an international sensation: in London a one-act comedy called *Where's Cruvelli*? was hastily put together and presented at the Strand Theatre. Meanwhile, Verdi seized his opportunity and asked Roqueplan, the director of the Paris Opéra, to release him from his obligations on the not unreasonable grounds that there was now not enough time to train a possible successor.

A few weeks later Cruvelli re-appeared as suddenly and as unexpectedly as she had left. 'She had been on a pre-marital honeymoon with her future husband Baron Vigier,' says Julian Budden succinctly. The Opéra management rejected Verdi's request and fired the unfortunate Roqueplan, whose job was taken over by Crosnier of the Opéra Comique. Verdi lost no time in complaining to him about Scribe's absence from rehearsals, his failure to make necessary adjustments to the text and the 'superior attitude' of some of the cast. Again he demanded to be released from the contract, but the dispute was somehow patched up and rehearsals resumed. However, as a result of Cruvelli's disappearance and subsequent difficulties the first performance of the new opera was delayed to coincide with the Great Exhibition of 1855.

Hector Berlioz had already been commissioned to write a *Te Deum* for the opening ceremony and a cantata for the close, but that an Italian opera should now be included among the celebrations created resentment among other French composers of the day. After the premiere on 13 June, wearing his critic's hat, Berlioz was among those who hailed the new work as a masterpiece. In a passage of soaring rhetoric, so typical of the period and so characteristic of the composer himself (one can almost hear the voice of Lélio), he refers to:

> . . . the penetrating intensity of melodic expression, the sumptuous variety, the judicious sobriety of the orchestration, the amplitude, the poetic sonority of his *morceaux d'ensemble*, the warm colours glowing everywhere and that sense of power, impassioned but slow to deploy itself, that is one of the characteristics of Verdi's genius, stamps the whole work with a grandeur, a sovereign majesty more marked than in any of the composer's previous creations.

What a pity they don't write them like that any more, even in France! Other critics praised the work in less extravagant terms. *La Presse* declared that 'Verdi's music has conformed to the procedure invented by French genius without losing anything of its Italian ardour', while in the *Assemblée Nationale* the composer Adolphe Adam said that he was impressed by the melodies and that the opera had converted him to Verdi's music as a whole. The Parisian public were no less enthusiastic; fifty performances of *Les Vêpres siciliennes* were staged during the first season.

To exploit the success Verdi immediately set about creating an Italian version. He was aware of the difficulties of making a good translation – words of one language rarely sit comfortably on music written for the words of another – but to protect his copyright he knew it was essential to have his own productions on the stages of Italian opera houses as quickly as possible. As he expected, the censors raised objections: an uprising in Sicily against established authority was considered far too inflammatory, and once again changes were demanded and the opera had to appear under unlikely titles. Not until Italian independence had been achieved, making possible the restoration of the original plot, did the work become known by its now-familiar title *I vespri siciliani*.

Nine separate and successful productions were staged in various parts of Italy during the carnival season of 1855-6. The opera was very well received, apart from the attractive *Four Seasons* ballet music, which, according to Muzio, was heard 'in icy silence.' This was probably less a comment on the quality of the music than a reflection of the taste of Italian audiences who, unlike the French, had no wish to see dances performed on an operatic stage. Like the splendid Overture, the ballet music written for *Les Vêpres siciliennes* is nowadays performed as a separate orchestral item from time to time.

During his two-year stay in Paris, Verdi twice visited London in an attempt to prevent clandestine performances of his music and to protect his copyrights. On both occasions Giuseppina went with him. She disliked the climate, the food and the fog as much as he had done, but she was impressed by the size of the city, the luxuries on display in the fashionable shops and the elegance of the menfolk. She tried to learn English, but without much success, as she confessed to a friend:

> . . . so far I have the consolation of not understanding a thing, not a single spoken word. These English wretches swallow half of what they say and the remainder they keep between their teeth; one would have to stay for a long time . . . to comprehend even a few sentences.

In the summer of 1855 Verdi took her to Enghien, near Paris, for the waters which were reputedly good for those with respiratory ailments. By the end of the year they had returned to Busseto, where Verdi plunged into his farming activities with obsessive zeal, and Giuseppina resumed her household and secretarial duties. Although she completely accepted Verdi's need for tranquillity and did her utmost to secure it, her mood slowly changed and she became bored by the routine at Sant'Agata and by their isolated life together. By degrees she began to over-eat and to take too little exercise, with the result that the trim and elegant figure of which she had once been so proud started to run to seed.

Verdi, on the other hand, was 'now in one of the few happy seasons of his life', in the words of the writer Feruccio Bonavia, who paints this picture of the composer in middle age:

> He had won something he prized more highly than fame or wealth – independence. Recognition was of course a first necessity, and even independence without it would have lost its sweetness . . . His position was now secure and he could return, after supervising a first performance at Milan or Paris, to the quiet life of Sant'Agata. When in residence there he would often go on market days to Busseto, to bargain with farmers and attend to the sale of stock he reared, of which he was very proud.

During their long stay in Paris there had been one important change on the domestic front which may well have appealed to Giuseppina's well-developed sense of irony as well as to her sympathetic nature. Not long after his wife died, Antonio Barezzi married a young maidservant called Maddalena, much to the fury of his family and the disapproval of many of his friends. Overnight he, too, became one of Busseto's social outcasts, which strengthened his bonds with Giuseppina and Verdi still further.

In the spring of 1856 Piave was invited to help with the re-working of
Stiffelio: 'Come quickly,' wrote Verdi, 'and, if you can, bring a poodle with
you, which you know will delight Peppina.' The librettist had never felt
entirely at ease at Sant'Agata, but he now found the house more
comfortable than before, and resigned himself to a long and busy stay. To
satisfy the more stringent demands of the censors it was decided to transfer
the main action of *Stiffelio* away from a contemporary Protestant sect to a
group of English crusaders of the 13th century. Their leader is Aroldo,
whose castle is 'near Kenth', and in the final scene there is a chorus for
Scottish huntsmen and shepherds assembled on the shores of 'Lago
Loomond': neither of these mis-spellings, it ought to be said, appears in
Verdi's original manuscript. The opera ends with a spectacular storm
which signals the reconciliation of Aroldo and his erring wife, Mina. The
first performance of *Aroldo* was not given until 16 August 1857, when it
was conducted by Angelo Mariani at a new opera house in Rimini, on the
Adriatic coast.

Meanwhile, in March 1856, Verdi spent a few days in Venice
supervising a revival of *La Traviata* at the Teatro La Fenice, whose
management asked him to write a new opera for production the following
year. He had turned down two previous offers because he was fully
occupied, or so he said, revising *Stiffelio* and *La battaglia di Legnano* and
with further exploratory work on *King Lear*. But now he declared himself
ready to take on a new commitment, and according to Gaia Servadio it
was Giuseppina who, once again, suggested a play by Antonio García
Gutiérrez, the author of *El Trovador*. This time the hero was a pirate from
Genoa, Simon Boccanegra, who rose to become the Doge of his city. All
the necessary ingredients were at hand: intrigue and treachery in high
places; cruel oppression and popular revolt; forbidden and secret love; a
long-lost illegitimate daughter and a devoted father.

Verdi's interest was immediately aroused, but it is curious that alarm
bells did not sound after his experience with *Il Trovatore*, for the plot of
Simon Boccanegra is even more complicated and improbable. He may
have been tempted by the great success of his first Gutiérrez-inspired
opera, but its successor is a dark and gloomy piece written by someone
'who seems to have had a mania for lost babies and mistaken identities' as
Dyneley Hussey observes. With so many twists and turns in the action it is
difficult to follow what is going on without a close knowledge of the
libretto. Verdi's contemporary, Abramo Basevi, who wrote one of the
earliest critical studies of the composer and his music, confessed that he
had to read through the original libretto no fewer than six times before he
could make any sense of it.

After the failure of the first performance in Venice the opera had a
mixed reception elsewhere. Productions in Rome, Reggio, Emelia and in
Naples in 1858 were fairly well received, but it failed miserably the
following year at La Scala and was laughed off the stage in Florence. The
Milan fiasco prompted Verdi's famous outburst to Tito Ricordi on the
nature of Italian audiences:

I accept their hisses on condition that I don't have to plead for their
applause. We poor gypsies, we charlatans – call us what you will – are
forced to sell our labours, our thoughts, and our dreams, for gold. For

SIMON BOCCANEGRA
Teatro La Fenice, Venice
12 March 1867
Revised version: Teatro alla Scala, Milan, 24 March 1881

Genoa in the mid-14th century: Simon Boccanegra, a corsair hero in the service of the Genoese republic, has fathered a child by the daughter of a local nobleman, Jacopo Fiesco. The child, a girl, disappears shortly after her birth, and Fiesco refuses to make peace with Boccanegra until she is found. Meanwhile, Boccanegra has been elected Doge by a group of plebeians led by Pietro and backed by a goldsmith, Paolo Albiani.

Twenty years later: Amelia, an orphan who has been brought up in the Fiesco household, is in love with the well-born Gabriele Adorno, but fears that she will be forced to marry Paolo Albiani. She meets Simon Boccanegra by chance and confides her anxieties to him. Amelia's replies to his questions convince Boccanegra, to his great joy, that she is his long-lost daughter. He thwarts Albiani's plans by refusing his request for Amelia's hand in marriage.

Not to be outdone the goldsmith arranges to have Amelia abducted, but she escapes. Simon Boccanegra, in return, forces the treacherous Albiani to call down a curse upon himself in the presence of the full Council. As a last act of revenge Albiani poisons Boccanegra who, before he dies, makes peace with Fiesco and blesses the union between Amelia and Adorno. His final request is that Gabriele Adorno should succeed him as Doge.

three lire the public buys the right to hiss or to applaud. Our fate is one of resignation, and that's all! But, whatever my friends or enemies say, *Boccanegra* is in no way inferior to many other operas of mine which were more fortunate . . .

The failure of a work on which he had set much store hit Verdi hard. What he seems not to have acknowledged, possibly because he was not consciously aware of the fact, is that in *Simon Boccanegra* he starts to move away from melodic supremacy and places more emphasis on dramatic expression than in any of his previous operas. We know that the need to experiment to find his own means of expression stayed with him all his life, but his contemporaries were mystified by new and 'progressive' elements. Some critics detected a growing influence of French grand opera: others, including Abramo Basevi, sought other explanations:

I would almost say, to judge at least from the Prologue, that he wanted to follow (albeit at a distance) the footsteps of the famous Wagner, the subverter of present-day music. It is well-known that Wagner would like to make music as determined a language as possible, almost the shadow of the poetry.

Simon Boccanegra was dropped from the repertoire when Verdi's next major opera *Un ballo in maschera* appeared in 1859, and might well have remained in obscurity, like *Stiffelio*, had it not been for the foresight and persistence of Tito Ricordi, the son of Verdi's publisher. For ten years or more he tried to persuade a reluctant composer to make major revisions, but it was not until 1880, when a collaboration with Boito came into view, that Verdi returned to the original score. 'It is not possible as it stands,' he admitted. 'It is too sad, too depressing.' Act II caused most concern because it lacked interest and vitality.

He recalled two letters Petrarch had written at the period in which the main action of the opera takes place, warning the people of Genoa and Venice, 'both sons of the same mother, Italy,' not to engage in fratricidal conflict. The poet thus reflected a sense of 'Italian motherhood' which, as Verdi said, 'was quite remarkable for that time.'

Such sentiments would go well in a Council scene, at which Paolo would be obliged to acknowledge his guilt. The character of Boccanegra would be enlarged to show statesman-like qualities as well as his natural, but more mundane, concerns for his daughter. Boito, who had likened the plot to 'a rickety table of which only one leg was sound', developed these ideas so effectively that he created one of the most dramatic scenes in the whole Verdi canon. This, and other changes he made, had a profound effect on the shape and structure of the original version. The extent of the revisions and their impact are even greater than those made previously to the first version of *Macbeth*.

When in the Spring of 1856 the secretary of the San Carlo in Naples, Vincenzo Torelli, offered Verdi a contract the composer suggested *King Lear*, provided suitable singers could be found. Marietta Piccolimini was approached to sing the key role of Cordelia, and it is quite possible that if the San Carlo had been able to agree terms with her, the long-cherished project would at last have come to fruition. Verdi had already chosen his librettist, one Antonio Somma, a lawyer/dramatist three years his senior,

A portrait of Giuseppina Strepponi painted in Naples, while *Un ballo in maschera* was being prepared. She told her friends that her pet dog Loulou recognized her at once!

he came to know while working on *La Traviata* in Venice.

There was a regular, if somewhat dilatory exchange of letters with the Neapolitan management, but Verdi left the contract unsigned while he put the finishing touches to *Simon Boccanegra*. Even after he had entered into a firm commitment with the San Carlo he continued to delay matters, having already made it clear that he was not prepared to have substitute singers 'imposed' upon him. Earlier he had asked Somma to have another subject ready, and as Naples grew increasingly restive he put forward a number of alternatives, including revivals of *Simon Boccanegra*, *Aroldo* and a revised *La battaglio di Legnano*. None of these proved acceptable.

In a mood of growing desperation he turned to an opera performed at the Paris Opéra twenty-five years earlier, with a libretto written by Eugène Scribe, entitled *Gustave III ou Le Bal masqué* (Gustave III or The Masked Ball). While Verdi dismissed Scribe's work as conventional and, at times, 'insufferable', he felt the subject itself was 'grandiose' and 'magnificent', and went on to give an assurance that Somma would be available to create an outstanding libretto from Scribe's material.

By this time the San Carlo management was ready to accept anything provided it was not merely a revival of an earlier work. And so it came about that a threadbare plot already used by at least three other composers, including Daniel Auber for whom it was written, emerged as Verdi's next project. Somma agreed to prepare the libretto, but under a pseudonym so he 'could write with more freedom'. The censors imposed many conditions and warned that the locale would have to be changed.

Of the original opera only the fatal *bal masqué* depicting the murder of Gustav III at the Stockholm Opera in March 1792, survived in the repertoire as a separate item, to be played as part of a mixed bill or on gala occasions. It was at one of these performances, on 13 January 1858, that an assassination attempt was made on Emperor Napoleon III and the Empress Eugènie. As the royal party made its way to the gala, bombs were thrown by a group of Italian revolutionaries led by Felice Orsini. Several people were killed, but the Emperor and his wife escaped. With some aplomb they carried on to the theatre, he with a ceremonial hat pierced by bomb splinters and she wearing a gown stained with blood. The evening's programme was suitably adjusted.

By a remarkable coincidence, the news of this outrage reached Naples on the very day Verdi arrived in the city with his new work – about an assassination of a reigning monarch in an opera house. The effect on the local Bourbon censors was entirely predictable. The composer had already reluctantly accepted many of their conditions, but now they failed to agree among themselves and in their panic called in the Chief of Police. He insisted on further cuts and changes so far-reaching that the work was completely undermined. The San Carlo sued for breach of contract, and Verdi countered by entering a claim for damages. After months of wrangling in the courts a compromise was reached: the management waived its rights to the new opera, and Verdi agreed to return to Naples in the autumn. *King Lear* came up once more but *Simon Boccanegra* was the final choice, with the baritone Filippo Coletti in the title role.

Meanwhile, Verdi looked for an alternative venue for his new opera. To Somma the obvious choice seemed to be Milan, where the censors were still reasonably relaxed, but the composer was more interested in Rome.

UN BALLO IN MASCHERA
Teatro Apollo, Rome
17 February 1859

Boston, towards the end of the 17th century: Riccardo, governor of the city, is in love with Amelia, the wife of his secretary, Renato. He is warned by a fortune-teller, Ulrica, that he will be murdered by the next man to shake his hand. Amelia guiltily responds to Riccardo's advances and seeks the advice of Ulrica, who prescribes a magic herb to quench her growing love for him. This has to be gathered by moonlight from a secret place near a scaffold, where she is joined first by Riccardo, who declares his love, and then by her husband who fails to recognize her under a black veil. On discovering the truth he joins a conspiracy to kill Riccardo and is chosen as the assassin. He follows his victim to a masked ball and shoots him. In his dying moments, Riccardo affirms Amelia's innocence and forgives those who have plotted against him.

That there was a play about Gustav III running in the city at that time may have had some bearing on his choice. The local censors were more lenient than had been expected: one or two expressions had to be altered, a few lines were cut here and there and, as in Naples, the locale had to be changed. Verdi suggested that the scene might be set in North America under English rule, or somewhere in the Caucasus. His librettist chose the first option, possibly because monarchy is regarded with less awe across the Atlantic than it is in Europe. All of which explains how, after a long and difficult transformation, Gustave III, King of Sweden, became Riccardo. Earl of Warwick (Conte di Warwich), governor of the city of Boston.

Most modern performances of *Un ballo in maschera* revert to the Swedish setting, but the original characters have to be retained as there is no way in which Verdi's music can be adjusted to accommodate Swedish names. The composer himself did not consider changes even when censorship in Italy came to an end. He was content to leave the action in Boston and made no attempt to revise his work, as he had done so often in the past. However, some of his admirers, and most of today's producers, seem unwilling to accept Verdi's implicit view that the music for his black comedy is more important than the setting. In an otherwise valuable essay by Benedict Sarnakar on the interaction between music and drama in the opera we find this observation:

> . . . the full dramatic force of the work depends on the royal status of the protagonist. If Riccardo were an ordinary citizen this would be a kitchen-sink tragedy, but as a king his personal weakness or virtue affects an entire community.

Julian Budden, among others, does not agree: he believes that the central issue in *Un ballo in maschera* is the chiaroscuro of Verdi's 'exquisitely fashioned' score. The contrasts between light and shade, day and night, love and remorse, friendship and conspiracy, cheerfulness and irony, virtue and vice – all these are realised and expressed in music that ranges from comic opera of great subtlety and distinction, recalling Offenbach or Sir Arthur Sullivan at their best, to the more familiar Verdi at the height of his menacing and melodramatic power.

Nowhere are these contrasts revealed more clearly than in the demanding role of Riccardo. As Peter Southwell-Sander reminds us, he is required to play many parts:

> . . . one moment the elegant courtier . . . light-hearted, then passion-
> ate; while in the scene with the fortune-teller . . . his singing has to
> match his sailor's disguise until he greets Ulrica's prophecy of his
> death with the laugh of a cynically-amused aristocrat.

Another notable role is that of Riccardo's page, Oscar, full of gaiety and wit, whose two arias reveal an aspect of Verdi's genius rarely seen.

The great Italian writer, adventurer and political leader, Gabriele D'Annunzio, once described *Un ballo in maschera* as 'the most operatic of all operas'. Pierluigi Petrobelli, Director of the Institute of Verdi Studies, does not go so far in acknowledging this often underrated work. Writing in the 1980s, he said that 'Never again would Verdi find the courage . . . to create tension between two poles so far apart. It is perhaps this which makes the opera so unique, and explains why we perceive this kind of musical theatre as so close to our sensibility.'

Chapter 10

The Forces of Destiny

After the collapse of the 1848 revolutions it was evident that Mazzini's idealism had failed, and the leadership of the *Risorgimento* passed to Camillo Cavour. He was the chief minister of the north-western state of Piedmont under Vittorio Emmanuele II, whose kingdom also included the island of Sardinia. Cavour was a realist, and knew that Austria, however slow-moving and bureaucratic, would always be able to crush any popular uprisings in its Italian dependencies.

A powerful ally had to be found, and the obvious choice was France under Emperor Napoleon III, who in his youth had served in the revolutionary army in Italy. He was now most unlikely to risk war with Austria or to support republicanism on his doorstep, however much sympathy he might feel towards the cause of the *Risorgimento*. Italian republicans, too, among them Garibaldi and Verdi, came to accept that that their country would stand a better chance of achieving freedom and unity under a constitutional monarchy than as a republic.

Early in January 1859 Vittorio Emmanuele II declared in the Piedmont parliament '. . . we cannot be insensible to the cry of anguish that comes to us from so many parts of Italy.' Within days Napoleon reached a secret politico-military agreement with Cavour and in March the Piedmontese army was mobilised.

Popular feeling ran high and in Rome, after a performance of *Un ballo in maschera* the slogan 'Viva *VERDI*', an acronym for '*Viva Vittorio Emmanuele Re D'Italia*', appeared on walls throughout the city. This ingenious idea spread like wildfire, and within days it became a rallying call all over the country. Verdi had been a popular figure for many years, but now he found himself treated once again as a national hero, one of the leaders of a movement which still had the unity and freedom of Italy firmly in its sights. He was sometimes cheered when he appeared in the streets, and wherever his operas were staged cries of *Viva Verdi*! and *Viva Italia*! could be heard above the excited applause.

Austria responded to the new provocations by demanding Piedmontese disarmament within three days – an ultimatum the wily Cavour was willing to accept if the Austrians were prepared to cede the heavily-fortified city of Piacenza. 'If the Italians want Piacenza,' was the blustering reply, 'they must come and get it'. Austria then declared war.

It was therefore in an atmosphere of mounting tension and excitement that Verdi and Giuseppina passed through Piacenza, where they stayed overnight in a hotel on the magnificent Piazza Grande, on a return journey to Sant'Agata. 'There was no avoiding the smell of war, the turmoil of guns and troops', says Gaia Servadio. On 30 April Austrian troops crossed the river Ticino to launch the invasion of Piedmont. It is said that Cavour heard the news while he was shaving, whereupon in a tuneless voice he burst into *Di quella pira*, Manrico's famous aria at the end of Act III of *Il Trovatore*.

True to his word, Napoleon sent in the French army to help the Piedmontese army and the growing bands of volunteers from various parts of Italy, while an independent force led by Garibaldi carried out diversionary attacks in Austrian-held Lombardy. Verdi, who had never completely trusted the French, wrote delightedly to the Countess Maffei:

> The miracles that have happened in these last few days! I seem hardly able to believe it all. Who could have expected such generosity from our ally? . . . I never believed the French would come to Italy or give their blood for us without thought of reward. I was mistaken on the first point; I hope to be equally mistaken on the second . . . I will ask a blessing on the 'great nation', I will henceforth willingly put up with their empty chatter, their polite insolence, and the contempt they have for everything that is not French.

In a series of battles – Montebello (20 May), Magenta (4 June) and Solferino (24 June) – the Austrian army was heavily defeated. During the early stages the fighting came perilously close to Sant'Agata, where Verdi and Giuseppina had stayed on after refusing to take refuge. The assiduous Mariani, writing from Genoa, kept them informed about the military and political situation. For a time there were fears for their safety: on 21 May, Giuseppina wrote to De Sanctis:

> We are in good health, not fearful but concerned about the serious events . . . This morning at eight o'clock the drawbridges were raised and the gates of Piacenza [roughly 18 miles away] were shut. A unit of the Franco-Piedmontese army is getting ready to attack the fortress and by tomorrow, or possibly by this evening, we shall hear the thunder of the guns . . . Verdi is serious, grave, but calm and confident about the future. I am certainly more anxious, more on edge, but then I am a woman and of a more nervous disposition.

In this letter, pledging De Sanctis to secrecy, Giuseppina revealed that she and Verdi had at last decided to marry. Whether the uncertainties of war had led them to this decision, or whether her entreaties had finally won the day is not known. It has even been suggested that Verdi, about to embark upon a political career, had thought it expedient to make an honest woman of Peppina, as she was affectionately known. A man may keep a mistress or two, but a politician ought to have a wife as well.

Later in the year, after the fighting had come to an end, the couple slipped away quietly to the tiny village of Collange-sous-Salève in the Piedmontese-held province of Savoy, near the Swiss border. The ceremony was conducted in the empty village church by the Abbé Mermillod after the local priest had been 'sent out for a walk' as Verdi put it. The two

Vittorio Emmanuele II (1820-1875), the first King of Italy.

witnesses were the resident bellringer and the coachman who had brought the marriage party from Geneva. Once the certificate was signed and dated 29 August 1859, husband and wife returned to Sant'Agata as quietly as they had left.

That they wanted a very private wedding is readily understood, but why cloak-and-dagger secrecy? If their aim was to silence gossip even at that late stage, why did they not make their marriage generally known? As matters stood few people were the wiser or the happier, with the exception of Peppina herself. She had achieved her life's ambition. She was now Signora Verdi, a respectable married woman, wife of the great composer and hero of the Italian people.

The euphoria felt by Italian patriots after the defeat of the Austrians turned to disappointment when they learned that Napoleon had met his brother Emperor, Franz Joseph of Austria, and had come to terms. Napoleon had had enough: 17,000 Frenchmen had died at Solferino, and politically he needed to protect his domestic flank. The military adventure had to come to an end.

Under the terms of their agreement Lombardy was to go to Piedmont, but Venetia, Mantua and Peschiera remained under Austrian control, and the position of all the other Italian states was virtually unchanged. Verdi was one of the many Italians who felt betrayed by the French Emperor:

> Now where is the longed-for and promised independence of Italy? . . . Such a downfall after so great a victory! All that blood for nothing! Poor, disappointed young manhood! And Garibaldi, who has gone so far to sacrifice his old and unwavering beliefs for the sake of a king, without purpose! It's enough to make one lose one's reason.

Cavour, too, opposed the treaty and resigned when the king signed it against his advice. He failed to see that Vittorio Emmanuele was more interested in extending his rule in northern Italy than in unifying the whole country. On his return to power Cavour lost popular support when, after a plebiscite, he ceded Nice and Savoy to the French as reward for their support in the war. After all the fine words, Napoleon had presented his squalid bill.

The treaty-makers had reckoned without the charismatic Garibaldi, who came from Nice and felt extremely bitter about Cavour's 'surrender'. In July 1860, having gathered around him a volunteer force of about 1,000 men, *i Mille* as they became known, he quietly sailed out of Genoa one night and made for the port of Marsala in Sicily, where popular unrest against the Bourbon monarchy had come to the surface once again. Fearing the embarrassing consequences of failure, Cavour sent gunships to intercept the two vessels carrying the tiny expeditionary force. Eluding their pursuers Garibaldi and his men landed at Marsala under the watchful eye of the Royal Navy, kept firmly shut in the finest Nelson tradition. Garibaldi declared his intention of fighting for 'Italy and Vittorio Emmanuele': volunteers in large numbers rallied to the cause, and within a month the Sicilian capital, Palermo, fell into his hands.

The world looked on with amazement as he drove the Neapolitans out of Sicily, crossed the Strait of Messina, captured Naples and marched north with a very much enlarged army to threaten the French-held Papal State and the city of Rome. To forestall a possible French or Austrian intervention Cavour sent Piedmontese troops to the scene, ostensibly to support Garibaldi but actually to prevent him capturing Rome. At the same time he tried to convince France and the other great European powers that the best chance of peace and stability in Italy rested with King Vittorio Emmanuele and his government.

The pieces were now in position for the endgame of the *Risorgimento*. Following the collapse of Austrian rule, the Romagna, Modena and Tuscany had already been ceded, while in Parma the people had also voted in favour of union with Piedmont and the Kingdom of Sardinia. Verdi was a member of the official delegation that formally conveyed the result of the plebiscite to Vittorio Emmanuele.

Garibaldi accepted the surrender of the King of Naples at Gaeta and

Giuseppe Garibaldi (1807-82), Italian patriot and leader of the *Risorgimento*.

promptly presented his two kingdoms, about half the total area of Italy, to Vittorio Emmanuele II exactly as promised and without conditions. In his book *Aspects of Verdi* George Martin pays this tribute:

> . . . in the supreme gesture of the *Risorgimento*, the purity of which made him the world's most popular hero of the nineteenth century, he refused any reward for his services. He would not accept from the king a title, a castle, a steamer, or even a dowry for his daughter. What he had done, he had done for Italy.

Cavour, who wanted Verdi in his new government as a prominent leader of the *Risorgimento*, persuaded him to stand as deputy for Busseto. The composer reluctantly agreed: after he was elected by a large majority he diligently attended meetings and followed Cavour's vote 'to be absolutely certain of not making a mistake.' But when Cavour died suddenly in 1861 Verdi lost interest: he completed his term of office but did not allow his name to go forward when the time came in 1865. To quote George Martin once more:

He was not a fatalist in the sense of believing that nothing a man can do will affect his fate. He believed in individual action, but he was also enough of a realist, or perhaps pessimist, to know that action is often ineffective and almost always costly.

It was in January 1861, while Verdi was away on one of his frequent visits to Turin, that a letter arrived at Sant'Agata from Giuseppina's old friend Mauro Corticelli, secretary of the actress Adelaide Ristouri who was at that time on tour in Russia. A second letter, from the tenor Enrico Tamberlick, was enclosed: both urged Verdi to consider accepting a commission from the Imperial Theatre of St Petersburg to write a new opera for their 1861-2 winter season. His music was extremely popular in Russia, they assured him, and his fee would be substantial.

Nothing less likely than Verdi's agreement seemed possible at that time. He had on more than one occasion declared his intention not to write another note of music. 'I am now the complete countryman,' he had told Piave: 'I hope I shall never be tempted to take up my pen again.' There was a time, as we have seen, when Giuseppina would have agreed with him wholeheartedly: but now, attracted possibly by the exciting prospect of a visit to Russia and bored once again by domestic routines, she had other ideas. She told her friends that she would do her best to persuade her husband to accept the proposal:

If eloquence does not do the trick, I will put into operation a method which I am assured works even with St Peter at the gates of Paradise . . . to make a nuisance of yourself until you get what you want. It is true that Verdi is less patient than St Peter, but if he packs me off to bed, never mind!

Attrition tactics were not necessary because Verdi was quite willing to consider the idea. He even suggested one of his favourite subjects, *Ruy Blas*, but a libretto inspired by Victor Hugo's story of a valet who became the lover of his Empress and rose to the rank of prime minister, was not considered by the Tsarist censors to be a topic suitable for presentation on the Russian stage, especially in the presence of his Imperial Majesty. Verdi's response reflected his integrity in such matters: he would not sign a contract until a subject had been agreed, but he would do his best to find a suitable alternative. While he was engaged upon this task his thoughts turned yet again to the richness of Spanish drama, and his final choice fell on *Don Alvaro*, or *La Fuerza del sino*, by Angel Pérez de Saavedra, Duke of Rivas.

The play had a colourful setting, was full of dramatic incident and sharply contrasted characters, and contained those elements of tragedy and comedy that Verdi considered essential to a successful libretto. As far back as 1853 he had said to Antonia Somma that 'our opera sins in the direction of too much monotony' and that he could no longer write on such subjects as *Nabucco* or *I due Foscari* because 'they lack variety'.

Having made his choice, which was accepted, a familiar sequence of events followed. Some minor characters and incidents were cut, although by no means all, and scenes were arranged and re-arranged many times. The services of Piave as librettist were secured, and the rows with him seemed an echo of the past:

> For God's sake, my dear Piave . . . We can't go on like this: it's
> absolutely impossible with this drama. The style must be tightened
> up. The poetry can and must say all that the prose says, but in half
> the number of words. So far, you are not doing that . . .

When Verdi rebuked his librettist in this manner at so early a stage of
their work together he unwittingly, perhaps, put his finger on the central
problem which faced them, and which faces producers of *La forza del
destino* even today. For it is the complexity of the opera that makes it
one of the most difficult of his works to stage. The characters are
rounded out and brilliantly portrayed; the orchestration shows ever-
increasing mastery and the thematic material is as strong as one could
wish, as the overture, written for the revised version, so clearly reveals.
But in his quest for variety, his determination to achieve a Shakespearean
richness with deeply-etched contrasts of light and shade, tragedy and
comedy, Verdi extends operatic form to its outermost limits. There is
variety in *Un ballo in maschera*, where the plot grows from scene to
scene and develops logically in a way that makes it almost credible. But
in *La forza del destino* Verdi takes this process much further. We move
abruptly from one colourful set piece to another. One moment we are
overwhelmed by the intensity of the drama; the next we are dazzled by
the brilliance of Preziosilla; impressed by the authority of Padre
Guardiano; amused by the pomposity of Fra Melitone; horrified by the

---

LA FORZA DEL DESTINO
Bolshoi Theatre, St Petersburg
10 November 1862
Revised version: Teatro alla Scala, Milan, 27 February 1869

Spain c.1740. Leonora, daughter of the Marquis of Calatrava, is about to elope with a young nobleman, Alvaro, when they are disturbed by her father. Alvaro accidentally kills him and the lovers flee for safety. The second scene opens 18 months later in an inn: among the crowd is Leonora's brother, Carlo, disguised as a student, who is pledged to avenge his father and kill his sister to restore family honour. He does not realise she is also there, dressed as a man, but she recognizes him.

A young gypsy girl, Preziosilla, sings in praise of war; some pilgrims arrive on their way to a nearby monastery; Leonora leaves in safety by joining their procession. On arrival she is barred by Fra Melitone but is seen by the Father Superior, Padre Guardiano, who allows her to live as a hermit, under the monastery's protection, to atone for her sins.

Later, in Italy, Alvaro has enlisted under an assumed name. Wounded in battle, he asks a comrade to destroy his box of private documents. The comrade is Carlo, also serving under a false name. He opens the box, finds his sister's portrait, and realises Alvaro's true identity. In the camp Preziosilla offers to tell fortunes and Fra Melitone, who has followed the regiment from Spain, rebukes the men for their sins. They chase him away. Carlo finds Alvaro and challenges him, but they are prevented from duelling by soldiers out on patrol.

Five years later Fra Melitone serves soup to the poor under the eye of the Father Superior, who tells him not to be envious if the beggars prefer to be helped by Fra Raphael, a recent arrival at the monastery. He is Alvaro, who has taken vows. Carlo tracks him down and taunts him: they leave holy ground to fight, by chance near Leonora's cave. Mortally wounded Carlo asks the hermit to hear his confession, but when he recognises his sister he stabs her to death. Alvaro curses destiny as Padre Guardiano commends Leonora's soul to heaven.

cruelty of Leonora's death at the hand of her dying brother.

These varied effects are not to be compared with those of a magic lantern show, which Verdi scorned, or of a Bombay film where the action regularly has to make room for attractive but irrelevant song-and-dance sequences. The variety on which Verdi insisted, and which he achieves in this opera, has a profoundly aesthetic aim. Like all great artists he fills the broadest canvas to portray, sometimes powerfully, sometimes poignantly, the tragedy and the comedy of human existence.

La forza del destino also reminds us that grand opera frequently means death to those taking part. 'It ain't over till the fat lady sings', might well be amended to read 'until the fat lady dies', so often is the stage littered with corpses as the final curtain comes down. Of course, violent death is by no means confined to opera: it runs like a thread throughout all classical and romantic literature cast in tragic mould. By convention, those most nobly born are those most at risk. Of the aristocrats in *La forza del destino* only Alvaro survives, and even he was killed off in the original version when he jumped from a cliff. But a noble death is not for common folk: most of us have to wait patiently to be overtaken by the infirmities and indignities of advancing years.

Giuseppina prepared for the journey to St Petersburg with enthusiasm, making sure that supplies of their favourite food and wine were sent in advance. When they reached the Russian capital by way of Paris and Berlin the cold 'was bitter . . . terrible', as she reported in one of her many letters, 'but the rich have managed to invent and procure the means to protect themselves from it.' The production of the new opera soon ran into difficulties: the *prima donna* fell ill and her understudy was a failure. The management of the theatre agreed with Verdi that the whole production should be shelved until the following year, when they would be in a better position to provide singers capable of doing justice to his many demanding roles.

No point was now to be served by staying on in St Petersburg, so the Verdis made their way back across Europe in February, at the coldest season of the year. At one stage of their travels they found themselves in an unheated railway carriage: ' . . . even the wine', Verdi complained, 'a good one at five roubles a bottle, turned to ice!' They broke their return journey at Paris so that he could represent Italy at the 1862 London Exhibition later in the year. He had previously agreed, with some misgiving, to compose a march for the opening ceremony, but when the time came he found that both Meyerbeer and Auber were providing similar pieces for their respective countries.

So he decided instead to write a cantata for solo voice, chorus and orchestra under the title *Inno alle nazione* (Hymn of the Nations) in which *La Marseillaise*, *God Save The Queen* and an Italian revolutionary song were to provide the climax. The young composer/poet Arrigo Boito, whose cause with Verdi the Countess Maffei had been carefully promoting for some time, was asked to prepare a text. While all this was happening Giuseppina went on ahead to London to enjoy its luxuries, shops and museums.

Controversy, never far from Verdi's side, arose when he was told that because his cantata 'was not in accordance with the terms of the commission' it could not be used at the opening ceremony, but that it

would be given a separate performance at Her Majesty's Theatre. The musical director and principal conductor at Covent Garden, Sir Michael Costa, who was known to be hostile to Verdi and jealous of his success, may have had a hand in this curious decision, or it may have been felt at Buckingham Palace that revolutionary songs were unlikely to amuse Queen Victoria. Another reason given officially was that a completely new work could not be properly learned or rehearsed in twenty-five days.

Verdi pointed out that an opera in its entirety could be learned in that time. He even wrote a letter to the editor of *The Times* making this known 'not to give importance to a matter of so little account, but only in order to correct the error that I did not deliver my composition.'

After the opening of the Exhibition he wrote to his French publisher, Léon Escudier:

What really carried the day was the *Marche* by Auber, to whom please give my regards and thanks, because without him I would have written a march . . . which would have bored the balls off me and everyone else.

Before closing the file on *Hymn of the Nations*, Verdi presented a watch to Arrigo Boito as a token of his thanks for the text. It was a gift much prized, for it marked the modest start of an uncertain, sometimes turbulent friendship that flowered in later years to become one of the most fruitful and important of all collaborations in operatic history.

Chapter 11

Exits and Entrances

La forza del destino took fashionable St Petersburg by storm, although a protest was mounted by demonstrators who considered that the fee paid to Verdi was beyond all reason. He had received 22,000 roubles, compared with the meagre 500 roubles offered to local composers for each of their operas. On the fourth night he was presented to the Tsar and showered with compliments, honours and decorations, including the Order of Saint Stanislaus. He and Giuseppina were overwhelmed by the warmth of Russian hospitality and the glittering social scene, and he sent regular reports to the Countess Maffei about Russia and Russian high society:

> You'll be amazed, amazed! In the past two months I've been frequenting salons, then there were suppers, parties and so on. I've met important and humble people, men and women of great amiability and exquisite *politesse*, quite different from the impertinent Parisian *politesse* . . .

With the opera itself, particularly the closing scene, Verdi was less than satisfied and decided that after meeting all existing commitments it would have to be withdrawn for substantial cuts and changes to be made. It was not until the La Scala production in 1869 that *Le forza del destino* appeared in the version usually heard today: Verdi's librettist was the editor of the Milanese journal *Gazzetta musicale*, Antonio Ghislanzoni, who went on to write the libretto of *Aida*.

Not long after their return from Russia the Verdis were on their travels again, this time to Madrid, where *La forza del destino* opened in Spain in the presence of the aged Duke of Rivas. They took the opportunity of touring Andalusia, and Verdi chose a cask of sherry for shipment to Sant'Agata to await their return. Meanwhile, they carried on to Paris, where he had a long-standing engagement to supervise a new production of *Les Vêpres siciliennes*. The visit was not a success. When the orchestra failed to turn up for an extra rehearsal he demanded an explanation from the conductor, who said they had other things to do. 'Other things to do than their duty?' roared Verdi, whereupon he grabbed his hat, stormed out of the Opéra and promptly left the city.

The return to the tranquillity of Sant'Agata suited him. He was able to strike a balance between his rural pursuits and his music, which continued to occupy much of his time. Nearly a third of the music for *Macbeth*, for example, needed to be re-written and there were other projects to be considered and the usual burden of administrative work. He also found himself in the centre of another row with the townspeople of Busseto who, in 1864, achieved their ambition of building a municipal opera house. When the idea was first mooted twenty years earlier Verdi supported it, but when work started in 1859 he felt that it should not be undertaken at a time of national emergency.

Now that the opera house built in his honour was ready many people, including his brother-in-law Giovanni Barezzi, felt that he should lend his support. His refusal, possibly in revenge for the malicious gossip of previous years, led to a violent quarrel with Barezzi. Eventually a compromise was reached: he paid 10,000 lire for a box in the theatre. But he never used it: not once did he set foot in the new building.

Giuseppina, whose enthusiasm for country life waxed and waned with the seasons, wanted him to compose again, as she told Escudier:

> For a very long time now I have heard him singing in all the keys, 'I don't want to write', and to be honest I am anxious that he should write because though I love the country very much, 365 days in it are too many – far too many! We have never stayed so long surrounded by these idiots . . . Once he is caught up the picture will change . . . he will give himself up to the fever of creation: he will devote himself fully to his text and his music and I hope the whole world will benefit from it.

Signora Verdi know her man well enough, but he believed that he was not ready to take on a major new commission. So when his publisher Escudier started to put out feelers on behalf of the Paris Opéra, the tone of Verdi's reply comes as no surprise:

> You must be joking! Me, write for the Opéra?!!! Do you really think I would be in no danger of having my eyes scratched out after what happened two years ago at the rehearsals of *Vêpres*?

Yet a fortnight later he was prepared to allow preliminary negotiations to go forward. The usual *King Lear* gambit was played, to which the director of the Paris Opéra, Emile Perrin, offered a choice of two possibilities – either *Cleopatra* or *Don Carlos*. Verdi rejected *Cleopatra*, but described *Don Carlos*, based on Schiller's poem of that name, as a 'magnificent drama' although 'a little lacking in spectacle.' And so it was agreed: the libretto to be written by the poet Joseph Méry and Camille du Locle, Perrin's son-in-law, and the opera to be ready for first performance during the Paris Universal Exhibition of 1867.

The only fault with *La forza del destino*, declares Julian Budden, is that it is an opera 'too rich in ideas. It is a fault on the right side.' Much the same can be said of *Don Carlos*, which is Verdi's longest and one of his most complex operas. It has often been suggested that both works may have influenced Mussorgsky when he composed *Boris Godunov*. The perils of absolute power; the destructive tensions between Church and State; the way in which the personal weaknesses and failings of those who rule can affect the lives of ordinary people – these are some of the basic themes that can be discerned in all three operas.

The complexity of *Don Carlos* is matched by the number of different

DON CARLOS
Académie Impériale de Musique, Paris
11 March 1867
In the mid-1560s, the heir apparent to the Spanish throne, Don Carlos, is to marry Elisabeth de Valois, daughter of the King of France. Theirs is a love match, but when King Philippe II decides to marry Elisabeth himself she reluctantly agrees in order not to jeopardize the newly-won peace between the two countries.

At the monastery where Charles V has either retired, or has died, the enlightened Rodrigo, Marquis of Posa, urges the King to lift the harsh Spanish regime in Flanders. The King hears his plea, but then tells Posa he suspects Elisabeth and Don Carlos of adultery. After an anonymous letter Don Carlos meets a veiled woman at midnight in the Queen's Gardens and, mistaking her for Elisabeth, declares his love. But she is the Princess Eboli, who feels betrayed when his error is revealed and threatens to inform Philippe II until dissuaded by the loyal Posa.

At a ceremonial burning of heretics Don Carlos defies the King and is arrested. Meanwhile, the Grand Inquisitor, alarmed by signs of growing unrest, demands exile or death for Don Carlos and the execution of Posa. The King accuses Elisabeth of adultery, but discovers that false charges have been made by Princess Eboli, who was at one time his mistress.

The Marquis of Posa is murdered by agents of the Inquisition as he visits Don Carlos in prison. Citizens rise up in his support but are quelled by the appearance of the Grand Inquisitor. In the confusion Eboli helps Don Carlos to escape. He bids farewell to Elisabeth as he prepares to leave for Flanders. Philippe II arrives to arrest him, but the gates open and Charles V, or a monk in his robes, takes Don Carlos into the safety of the cloister.

versions that exist, each with its own juxtapositions, additions and deletions, some made with Verdi's approval, others not. Even today there is no single standard edition, although most modern productions follow a five-act version which includes a magical introductory scene set in the forest of Fontainebleau. This, for unfathomable reasons, was struck out before the first performance.

After long neglect, the opera has enjoyed a revival in recent years. Productions have been given in French, in which the libretto was written, and parts of the original score have also been restored, including a duet between Don Carlos and his father which Verdi used later, in 1874, in the *Lacrimosa* of the *Requiem*.

As we have seen, Verdi's concern for historical accuracy was no greater than that shown by Schiller, but this does not explain how he came to accept a basic departure from the original plot in the libretto prepared by Joseph Méry and Camille du Locle. Schiller's dramatic poem reaches a powerful climax when the King hands over his son to the Grand Inquisitor with the terrible words 'Cardinal, I have done my duty. Do yours.' There can be few more effective or chilling curtain lines.

However, this impact is entirely lost in the final scene of the opera. Unless the producer imposes his own solution, the audience is left to work out what is happening on stage. *Don Carlos* is essentially an opera of ideas, but nevertheless it is difficult to understand how Verdi, with his feel for the theatre and his own highly-developed dramatic instinct, could have allowed Schiller's crystalline *dénouement* to be replaced by such a shadowy conclusion, so full of ambiguity and mystery.

Before he started work on *Don Carlos* Verdi had agreed to take a winter residence on the coast, mainly for the sake of Giuseppina whose health was affected by the short, bitterly cold seasons at Sant'Agata. Their large and well appointed new apartment was in the Palazzo Sauli on the hill of Carignano, overlooking the port of Genoa. It had been chosen by Mariani who, without consulting them, took an adjoining suite of five rooms presumably as a reward for having negotiated the deal. He made it quite clear that he would pay a proper rent for this sub-lease and that he would take care of the Verdis' apartment while they were away.

Giuseppina cannot have looked upon this arrangement with any great enthusiasm as she trusted Mariani no more than any other member of her husband's circle of friends. However, she was glad to escape the dreary snows of Sant'Agata and threw herself with enthusiasm into the task of furnishing 'her fifth and final home' as she put it. It was consoling activity, for she had still not fully recovered from the death in 1862 of her beloved pet dog, Loulou. 'Four days of atrocious suffering,' she had written to a friend, 'have brought him to everlasting rest under a weeping willow in our garden.' Verdi himself had buried the animal, and had placed a marble slab over its grave. The following year Camillo, her illegitimate son, died at the age of twenty-five in Siena. He was an apprentice doctor who had gone to help deal with a cholera epidemic in that city. It is probable that he became infected and lost his life treating others. What Giuseppina felt about the loss is not known.

Verdi composed the third act of *Don Carlos* at the Palazzo Sauli and then took Giuseppina with him to Paris to complete the opera. There followed a brief holiday in the Pyrenees and then a return to Paris to supervise the preparations for the first night. While they were away from home Italy became involved in the Austro-Prussian war and suffered a series of humiliating defeats on land and sea at the hands of the Austrians. However, Prussian might prevailed, and the Italians received Venice and the Veneto as payment for their support, much as a dog might receive titbits from the table for good behaviour. National self-esteem suffered further blows when cholera epidemics broke out in many of the major cities, and civil unrest flared up once more in Palermo. 'Verdi is in a very black mood, and so am I', confided Giuseppina. 'At this moment no Italian with any heart can be happy or calm in spirit.'

Don Carlos had a mixed reception on its first night in Paris. At one point, when the King tells the Grand Inquisitor to hold his tongue (*Tais-toi, prêtre*) the Empress Eugènie, the staunchest of Catholics, rose to her feet and turned her back on the performance. Verdi, firmly convinced that he had produced his finest opera to date was in no way discouraged by the lukewarm reception, neither was Angelo Mariani, who determined to stage an Italian version, *Don Carlo*, in Bologna as soon as possible. While he was working on this production Verdi learned of his father's death. The old man, in his eighties, had been ill for some time; nevertheless Verdi was 'stricken with grief', as we learn from Giuseppina. She went on to say that although she and her father-in-law 'were poles apart in their thinking' she felt 'profoundly sorrowful . . .'

After the Bologna production Verdi returned to Sant'Agata, making life difficult for his foreman Paolo Marenghi. His employees were unable to escape his black moods, unlike Giuseppina, who managed to get away to Milan on shopping expeditions. On one such occasion that she decided to

visit the Countess Maffei. The two ladies had not previously met but they got on extremely well – to such an extent, in fact, that together they went to pay a social call on the aged poet and novelist Alessandro Manzoni, author of *I promessi sposi* (The Betrothed). The old man was charmed by his visitors, and gave Giuseppina a self-portrait for her husband: on the back of the photograph he wrote, 'To Giuseppe Verdi, a glory of Italy, from a decrepit Lombard writer.'

In July 1867, Antonio Barezzi died. 'For some days,' writes Gaia Servadio, 'Verdi remained totally silent, wandering around Sant'Agata, tired and ill: the death of Barezzi, the man to whom he owed so much was not to be endured.' In a touching letter to Clarina Maffei, Verdi said:

'You know that I owe him everything, everything, everything . . . what generosity, what heart and virtue he had. I've known many men, but none better than he. He loved me as one of his own sons, and I loved him as much as my father.' A dramatic account of the death of Barezzi appears, among other places, in *The Letters of Giuseppe Verdi*, selected and translated by Charles Osborne:

> When the end came, Verdi and Giuseppina were with him. Barezzi was in bed, weak and hardly able to speak, but he raised his eyes longingly to the piano which stood in the corner of his room. Verdi understood that he was asking for his favourite tune from *Nabucco*, so he sat and began to play '*Va, pensiero*'. Barezzi raised his hand, murmured 'Oh, my Verdi', and died peacefully.

The sombre year exacted a further toll in December, when Piave suffered a stroke which deprived him of movement and speech, but left him otherwise conscious and able to recognize people. For eight years he lingered in this pitiful condition, his two main concerns being the future of his daughter and his dependence on Verdi, who helped him with money. The composer also organised for his benefit the publication of a group of six songs by various composers, including Mercadante, Auber and Thomas. His own contribution was *Stornello*, set to an anonymous text.

Gioacchino Rossini died in Paris on 13 November 1868: the two men had known and admired each other for many years. Their letters had an easy, bantering tone: even in his darkest moods Verdi – 'of a melancholy cast of mind', as Rossini once put it – rarely failed to respond to his friend's wit and good humour. Verdi, for his part, once described *The Barber of Seville* as 'the most beautiful *opera buffa* in existence.' He sent the following letter to the editor of the *Gazetta musicale*:

> To honour the memory of Rossini, I should like to ask the most distinguished Italian composers (Mercadante above all, if only for a few bars) to compose a Requiem Mass to be performed on the anniversary of his death. I should like not only the composers but also the performers to give their services free and to contribute a modest amount towards the expenses. The Mass should be given in the Church of San Petronio in Bologna, which was Rossini's real musical home . . . after the performance it should be sealed and placed in the Music Academy of that city.

Verdi led the way by composing a final section, *Libera me*, for soprano, full chorus and orchestra. However, the local impresario in Bologna

declined to make his singers and orchestra available without payment, and
other difficulties arose. Verdi felt that Mariani was partly to be blame: he
'has not lifted a finger in this affair which I so recommended to him. [We]
can only do one thing: restore the pieces to the various composers and say
no more about it.' Some believed that Mariani was offended when he was
not asked to be one of the composers, only to conduct the work. Thus the
first cloud appeared over the friendship between the two men that Mariani
had been at such pains to cultivate. The storm followed later.

The various parts of the Rossini Mass were recently recovered and the
work performed for the first time at the Stuttgart Festival in 1988, with
Helmuth Rilling conducting. Not surprisingly, it is a work uneven in
quality and one which has rarely been heard since, but it inspired Rilling
to commission a *Requiem of Reconciliation* to mark the 50th anniversary
of the end of World War II. Composers from fourteen countries were
invited to take part and at the premiere in the Stuttgart Liederhalle the
Israel Philharmonic Orchestra under Rilling was given a 20-minute
ovation.

After the collapse of the Rossini initiative Verdi had to attend to more
immediate commitments such as the major revision of *La forza del destino*
for La Scala. Now that Piave was no longer available the versatile Antonio
Ghislanzoni, editor of the *Gazzetta musicale*, was invited to amend the
libretto. Versatile is hardly the word, for few music journalists can have
had a more colourful career. After starting life as a medical student and
taking up the double bass, he became a professional singer and finally a
full-time writer. He once created a stir in the large square in front of Milan
cathedral by appearing as an ancient Roman general: he had forgotten to
change his costume after a performance. A genuine eccentric who had little
regard for the social conventions of the day, his musical knowledge,

writing skills and long experience of the theatre made him an ideal choice as collaborator.

Much to Verdi's satisfaction the February 1869 production of *La forza del destino* was well received. Press and public were unanimous in their praise, and the long-standing feud between the composer and La Scala was quietly buried. Later in the year he was appointed Cavaliere to the Order of Merit of Savoy: usually he paid little heed to honours but he was touched by this recognition from his fellow-countrymen and gave the annual pension of 600 lire to needy pupils at his old school in Busseto.

Among the many proposals for new works were some from du Locle in Paris. Impresario, composer and their wives became good friends during the *Don Carlos* rehearsals and when the Verdis returned to Paris in March 1870 the du Locles and Emanuele Muzio were among the first people they called on. Since their previous visit, Camille du Locle had become manager of the Opéra Comique and Verdi was impressed by what he saw. It was at this time that the director of the new opera house in Cairo, Draneht Bey, asked Verdi to write an ode for the official opening. The invitation was politely refused, and a production of *Rigoletto* marked the occasion instead. The next approach came from an agent of the Khedive, Ismail Pasha, who offered the most generous terms for a new opera to celebrate the forthcoming opening of the Suez Canal, an enterprise with which the French were much involved at that time. Again Verdi declined the offer, but du Locle followed up by sending him a 'printed sketch' which 'he ought to read'. Verdi found it 'absolutely first-rate' and asked du Locle to come to Sant'Agata to discuss the scenario. He asked if Ghislanzoni would be available to write the libretto, for which he would be well paid. 'But do not talk about this matter,' Verdi warned, 'as a contract has yet to be signed.'

The author of the 'printed sketch' was an Egyptologist, Auguste Mariette, who had been sent to Egypt by the French government in 1850 to acquire ancient manuscripts. He settled in the country, made a number of archaeological discoveries, became Curator of Ancient Monuments and was given the honorary title of 'Bey' by the Khedive. There was a cunning postscript to his covering letter to du Locle:

If M. Verdi does not accept, His Highness begs you to knock at another door . . . Gounod and even Wagner are being considered. The latter, if he would be willing, could write something really grand.

Under the contract Verdi was to receive four times the substantial sum he had been paid for *Don Carlos*. He insisted the actual figure should remain secret 'in order not to disturb the underpaid ghosts of Mozart, Beethoven, Schubert and Rossini.' As soon as terms were agreed du Locle withdrew, but not before he had made valuable contributions to the text, and his place was taken by Ghislanzoni, who threatened to bring with him a Nubian slave whose limbs could be fed to the three mastiffs guarding the gates of Sant'Agata while he passed safely through.

Work began without delay, and in four months *Aida* was virtually complete. Verdi himself wrote the words of *Celeste Aida*, 'a romanza to be added at the tenor's pleasure'. Many letters written by Verdi to Ghislanzoni survive (but unfortunately not the replies) which throw light on their working methods and the composer's astonishing attention to

Antonio Ghislanzoni (1824-93) wrote the libretto of *Aida*, and helped to revise *La forza del destino* and *Don Carlos*.

detail. After a careful analysis of part of the duet between Aida and Amneris in Act II he says that 'when the action requires it I should abandon rhythm, rhyme and strophe altogether . . . there are moments in the theatre when poets and composers must have the talent to write neither poetry nor music.'

Ghislanzoni accepted Verdi's instructions without question, but he was sufficiently confident to make suggestions on his own account. He was also better at sticking to promised dates than many of his predecessors and replied promptly to letters: qualities of a good journalist to which Verdi attached great importance. But, as always, he pounced like a tiger if there were any signs of backsliding, as shown by this extract from a note dated 8 September 1870:

> . . . The last words of your letter sent a shudder down my back. 'I can let you have the beginning of the third act.' How is this? Isn't it finished? I am waiting for it from hour to hour. I have completed the second act. Send me the text as soon as possible. Meanwhile, I will do some polishing here and there . . .

Other letters of even greater length followed at frequent intervals, so long and so frequent that one wonders how Verdi ever found time to write

AIDA

Opera House, Cairo

24 December 1871

The action takes place at Memphis and Thebes during the time of the Pharaohs. Ramfis, High Priest of Egypt, tells general Radames that the Ethiopians have invaded their country, and that the goddess Isis has chosen a 'brave young warrior' to lead the Egyptian army against them. Ramfis leaves Radames wondering whether he is the one who has been named. He dreams of the glory to be won in victory, and then his thoughts turn to the beautiful Aida (*Celeste Aida*) with whom he is in love. She is an Ethiopian bound in slavery to the princess Amneris, daughter of the Pharaoh, who is also in love with Radames. She guesses correctly that Aida is her rival, but like everyone in the Egyptian court she does not know that Aida is, in fact, also a princess, daughter of Amonasro, King of Ethiopia. Pharaoh enters with his court; news comes that the Ethiopians are approaching; Radames is revealed as the chosen leader and Amneris tells him to return victorious – (*Ritorna vincitor*). There follows the famous scene at the end of Act I in which the High Priest and others call down blessings on the expedition, invoking the power of 'mighty Phtha'.

Amneris taunts Aida by telling her that Radames has been killed in battle, and then reveals not only that is he alive but also that she loves him. Aida begs for pity, but Amneris thinks only of vengeance. The sound of trumpets is heard, signalling the defeat of the Ethiopian army. Amneris places a victory crown on the head of Radames, who asks that the lives of the prisoners should be spared. His wish is granted but, at the insistence of the priests, the reprieve does not extend to Amonasro who is among the prisoners, disguised as a junior officer.

By moonlight, Amneris and the High Priest make their way to a temple on the banks of the Nile. Aida arrives for a secret tryst with Radames, and sings of her deep longing for her beloved country, (*O patria mia*). Amonasro appears and, appealing to Aida's patriotism and sense of duty, persuades her to trick Radames into revealing his military plans so that the Ethiopians can avenge their defeat. Radames at last arrives and towards the end of the great love duet he tells Aida the route the Egyptian army proposes to take. Overhearing this, Amonasro emerges from hiding, reveals his true identity and together with Aida urges Radames, appalled by what he has done, to flee the country with them. Before he can decide, however, Amneris and the High Priest come out of the temple. Radames gives himself up to them, as Aida and her father escape.

The scene changes to a great hall in the Palace, where Amneris tries in vain to persuade Radames to marry her to save his life. He is led away for judgement, and a desperate Amneris reviles herself as the verdict of the court of priests is awaited. Finally the voice of Ramfis is heard pronouncing sentence: the culprit is to be buried alive under the temple of Isis, the deity he has offended. Aida is determined to die with him and secretly hides in the tomb beforehand. The opera ends with their great duet 'O terra addio', as Amneris, dressed in mourning, weeps and prays in the temple above, and the priestly chorus chant their strange invocations to the mighty Phtha.

the music. An entire chapter could, with advantage, be devoted to a closer examination of these shavings from the workshop floor. 'We must have the smell of Egypt in our nostrils . . . We must find a newer form.'

The words of the final duet, *O terra, addio* are entirely his own work. He wrote them 'to make my meaning clear' and asked for improvements. However, when Ghislanzoni replied he was told that his verses were 'beautiful, but not quite right for my purposes'. Verdi went on to explain that 'in order to save time' he had by now written music to his own 'monstrous' text. To pursue the workshop metaphor, in *Aida* the marks of Verdi's chisel are everywhere to be seen. The music is the most direct expression of his genius, of course, but so much of the text was also his work, or was written by other hands under his inspiration and control, that it is no exaggeration to say that not one but four librettists were involved in the opera.

August Mariette wrote the original outline of the plot, du Locle helped to develop the scenario, Ghislanzoni wrote the verses, but it was Verdi who held in his hands the balance between words and music – one of the great glories of the opera. Once the story and its exotic setting had seized his imagination the vision of the work as a whole was clearly in his mind, but this did not prevent him from paying attention to the smallest detail in the music, in the text or in the production. It was characteristic of his genius that it worked at every level, and at all times, to bring *Aida* so triumphantly to the operatic stage.

Triumphantly – but late, because all the costumes and sets were held up in the Siege of Paris during the autumn and winter of 1870-71. When the Franco-Prussian War broke out in July it was widely believed that the French would win easily, but in September they were heavily defeated at Sedan. A bloodless revolution followed in Paris, a republic was declared and the Prussians laid siege to the city. The Empress Eugènie, the Prince Imperial and other members of the French royal family were allowed to slip quietly away to exile in England, where they were later joined by the ailing Emperor Napoleon III who had been captured at Sedan with most of his army. For the first two or three months the ordinary people of Paris treated the siege as a joke, but as the winter set in conditions deteriorated rapidly. Intense cold, starvation and disease took a growing toll of the population; animals in the Paris Zoo were slaughtered for food, and dogs, cats and even rats, disappeared from the streets. Worse was to follow under the rule of the Commune, who shot the Archbishop of Paris and other hostages and burned down a number of public buildings. Sharing the many dangers and hardships were the unfortunate Mariette and his family, who found themselves trapped with all the lavish *Aida* scenery and the splendid costumes on which his expert advice had been sought.

In the wider world outside, the defeat of France enabled Vittorio Emmanuele II to complete the unification of Italy. His forces occupied the Papal States after the French withdrawal, leaving only the Vatican City as a small enclave with independent status. This final action in the long struggle for Italian unity left Verdi unmoved, although he acknowledged its importance. He was by now more concerned about the fate of France, the land 'that gave liberty and civilization to the modern world. If she falls,' he wrote, 'let us not deceive ourselves that all our liberty and civilization will fall too.' From his advance on *Aida* royalties he asked du Locle to give two thousand francs immediately to help French soldiers wounded in battle.

When the siege of Paris came to an end preparations began in earnest for the premiere of *Aida* in Cairo, which took place on 24 December 1871. Mariani had been engaged to conduct the performance, but by then the breach with Verdi had become open and bitter. Muzio was enlisted as a replacement, but was unable to keep the engagement when the time came, and it fell to Giovanni Bottesini, a double bass player with the Italian Opera in Cairo, to conduct the work in public for the first time. It was a huge success, but Verdi was not there to enjoy it. He recoiled from the

The opening four bars
of *Celeste Aida* in
Verdi's own manuscript.

huge amount of publicity that surrounded the opening of the Canal and the celebrations that went with it.

The opening of *Aida* in Milan, however, was an event to which Verdi attached the greatest importance. A close friend of Boito, Franco Faccio – a young rebel won over to Verdi's cause and now one of the finest interpreters of his music – conducted the first European performance of the new opera, which overwhelmed the public and most of the critics. There were a few complaints about Wagnerian influences, which irritated Verdi, but generally he was well satisfied with the reception.

The formidable soprano Teresa Stolz, Bohemian by birth and by temperament, scored a notable success in the title role. She had originally been chosen for the premiere in Cairo but had stayed behind in Milan at the composer's request, or so it was suggested at the time. A strikingly handsome woman in her early forties, Donna Leonora was her first major role in a Verdi opera in the revised version of *La forza del destino*. She became Mariani's mistress, and when she moved into his apartment at the Palazzo Sauli in Genoa she also became, by proxy as it were, a close neighbour of the Verdi household. She was as ambitious as she was gifted, and malicious tongues soon put it about that she intended to desert Mariani for the composer, who was highly flattered to receive the attentions of a younger woman.

How much of this gossip, and all that followed, was false and how much based on fact we shall probably never know. Certainly, they were seen in public together frequently and addressed each other in familiar terms. But such behaviour is commonplace in the musical and theatrical worlds of today, even in Anglo-Saxon countries, where a word such as 'darling' is used more often as a form of address than as a term of endearment. Teresa Stolz was a frequent guest at Sant'Agata where she seems always to have received a warm and friendly welcome from Giuseppina as well as from Verdi himself. It was on their advice that she broke off her liaison with the ailing Mariani: not the sort of counsel one would expect Giuseppina to endorse, even at her most devious, if she were a wronged wife.

Biographers are at odds with each other on this issue. At one end of the scale is Frank Walker, who says firmly that 'there is no evidence at all that there was an affair between Verdi and the singer', quoting some of Giuseppina's letters to prove his point. At the other end is Gaia Servadio who claims that Verdi was in love with Stolz 'whether he knew it or not.' Just as she had earlier suggested that a subconscious link exists in the case of *La traviata* between Violetta and Giuseppina, she asks us to accept that in Aida the heroine, 'who holds the heart of Radames, was a metaphor for Teresa Stolz; while Giuseppina in the Amneris role smoothly treats her as a friend . . .' This ingenious idea does not square with Verdi's original intention that Antonietta Fricci should sing Aida in the Milan production, with Teresa Stolz as Amneris. It was only later, and on Ricordi's recommendation, that Verdi agreed to change the roles, choosing the young, beautiful, fairly inexperienced Austrian mezzo-soprano, Maria Waldmann, to play opposite Stolz.

Other writers take their stand on safer, higher ground when they say that we shall probably never know whether Verdi and Stolz were lovers. Surely it is a matter of no importance other than to those concerned. To

Teresa Stolz, from a
pastel sketch by
Gariboldi in the
Museum of La Scala,
Milan.

which we might add that even if the truth were suddenly to be revealed to us at this late hour, it would add little to our understanding of Verdi the man, and nothing at all to our understanding or appreciation of his music.

Chapter 12

'My Farewell To You All . . . '

After the success of *Aida* at La Scala, other opera houses were eager to mount productions of the new opera. Verdi received many invitations to attend opening nights, most of which he declined, pointing out that his presence would have no effect on the performance and that he had no wish to be on public display. However, he attended a first night in Parma, possibly because he felt he ought to acknowledge the plaudits of his fellow-citizens. He also insisted on being present in Naples in March 1873, because he still lacked confidence in the San Carlo management and because it was a city he enjoyed visiting.

As it happened he had time on his hands: Teresa Stolz had fallen ill and the opening night had to be postponed. To keep himself amused he composed a string quartet in E minor – an agreeable, elegantly written work, classical in form. It was performed in Verdi's hotel for a small group of friends after the first night of *Aida*. He then did his best to suppress the quartet, saying it was not intended for public performance: in the end he had to bow to public demand and four years later allowed Ricordi to publish.

Verdi was on his travels again in May 1873 when he heard of the death of Alessandro Manzoni, the last of his heroes, at the age of eighty-nine. When he met the poet for the first time he had been touched by his simple manner. 'Now all is over,' he said to Clarina Maffei: 'with him ends the most pure, the most holy, the greatest of our glories.'

He did not attend Manzoni's funeral in Milan, but visited his grave a few days later to pay silent homage with Clarina Maffei and Ricordi. Through his publishers, on 'an impulse or, rather, heartfelt necessity', he offered to compose a Requiem Mass for the first anniversary of the poet's death. He was willing to pay for printing the music if the city authorities funded the performance. His offer was accepted, although some members of the Milan City Council objected that the money would be better spent helping the poor. Thanks largely to Boito's powers of persuasion the vote went in favour, and Verdi decided to set aside time to work on the score during his summer holiday with Giuseppina in Paris. Shortly after Manzoni's funeral, Clarina Maffei heard from Giuseppina:

In a few days, I think Verdi will actually make another journey to Milan but I will stay in Genoa. He has many things to arrange for his

Mass . . . It's true that when one reaches a certain age, one lives on memories. We all have happy ones and sad ones and fond ones but, alas, not everyone is fortunate enough to keep affections and friendships intact . . . I tell you with deep disappointment that I don't believe in anything any more and almost nobody . . . my religious faith has disappeared and I cannot quite believe in God even when I look upon the marvels of Creation!

The letter ends on this melancholy note: 'my friendship is worth nothing, but if you don't ignore it, I have the honour to claim myself to be your affectionate Giuseppina Verdi'.

The reasons for her low spirits are not hard to find: her health was poor, she was prematurely aged, there were frequent quarrels with her husband, and now that regular visits by Teresa Stolz had turned her household into a virtual *ménage à trois*, suspicion could never have been far below the surface, however skilfully she managed to hide her feelings. As we have seen, she disliked some of Verdi's friends and distrusted others, but – reminded no doubt of her own mortality – she was deeply depressed by the fate overtaking so many of them. The rejected Mariani was dying of cancer, alone in his flat, du Locle and Léon Escudier had been made bankrupt by the recession after the Franco-Prussian War; De Sanctis could not repay the money he owed to Verdi, losing his respect. The future held another blow: Mauro Corticelli, Giuseppina's trusted friend, the bailiff at Sant'Agata, was to be sacked for dishonesty and attempted suicide a few days later in Milan.

Verdi, now in his sixties, continued to flourish. His vitality and creative powers were undimmed, and when he settled down to composition he did so with relish. It has been said that after *Aida*, disenchanted with the operatic world, he thought of giving up writing operas and turning to other forms, including choral music, as Rossini had done. One commentator claims that he had started to compose a Requiem Mass *before* Manzoni died, but the evidence is inconclusive.

We know he kept his contribution to the unperformed Rossini Mass, the *Libera me*, in the form of a double fugue, which became the closing section of the Manzoni *Requiem*. As he said to the professor of music at the Milan Conservatorio, some parts of the work are reprised in the *Libera me*. So there is no doubt, despite Dyneley Hussey's contrary view, that Verdi had glimpsed the possibility of a larger work that would find its fulfilment in the section already composed.

Well before he finished the work, preparations began for its first performance on 22 May 1874 in the Church of San Marco, the only church in Milan where women were allowed to sing. Teresa Stolz, to whom Verdi later presented his manuscript, and Maria Waldmann took the soprano and mezzo-soprano parts, with Giuseppe Capponi and Armando Maini as tenor and bass respectively: chorus and orchestra were conducted by the composer. The day before the performance, in the *Allgemeine Zeitung*, the well-known German conductor and critic Hans von Bülow, described the *Requiem* as Verdi's 'latest opera, though in ecclesiastical robes' – a foolish canard which persists to this day. Brahms roundly declared that 'Bülow has made an almighty fool of himself. Only a genius could have written such a work.' Eighteen years later, Bülow made amends in a letter dated 7 April 1892:

The Manzoni *Requiem* was first performed in the Church of San Marco, Milan. This sketch was made during one of the subsequent performances at La Scala, and shows Maini, Capponi, Waldmann and Stolz under the direction of the composer.

Deign to hear the confession of a contrite sinner! . . . A recent performance of the *Requiem*, though it was a poor one, moved me to tears. I have studied it not only according to the letter which kills, but according to the spirit which quickens. And so, illustrious master, I have come to admire you and to love you! Will you absolve me and exercise the royal prerogative of forgiveness?

And much more in this style, to which Verdi sent a dignified reply:

There is no shadow of sin in you, and there is no need to talk of penitence and absolution. If your opinions have changed, you have done well to say so; not that I should have dared to complain. For the rest, who knows? . . . perhaps you were right in the first instance.

The *Requiem* was so successful that three more performances had to be given at La Scala. The Verdis and the four soloists then set off for Paris, where seven performances met with 'apparently genuine success' at the Opéra Comique. At the end of June Verdi visited London, declined Covent Garden's proposal to present the *Requiem* and *Aida* in the same concert, rejected the Crystal Palace as a venue on account of its poor acoustics, and chose instead the recently-built Royal Albert Hall for the London premiere of the *Requiem*. He then returned to Sant'Agata, leaving Giuseppina to supervise a move to the Palazzo Doria, their new winter home in Genoa. In November he was nominated Senator in the Italian Parliament, a purely titular honour, and later the government of the new French republic

awarded him the Cross of the *Légion d'Honneur*.

On 15 May 1875 he returned to London to conduct the *Requiem* but, according to Julian Budden, 'the performance was poorly attended . . . Verdi had reckoned without the Puritanism of the Victorians, who liked their liturgical music solemn and sedate. Mawkishness they could tolerate: theatricality never.' In view of the losses a performance in Berlin was cancelled, but consolation was found in Vienna where audiences responded to the work with enthusiasm. Of the many reviews that appeared as the *Requiem* made its way across Europe, few contained comments more apposite than those made by Giuseppina:

> They talk a lot about the more or less religious spirit of Mozart, Cherubini and others. I say that a man like Verdi must write like Verdi, that is according to his own way of feeling . . . The religious spirit and the way in which it is expressed must bear the stamp of its period and its author's personality. I would deny the authorship of a Mass by Verdi that was modelled upon the manner of A, B or C.

'For the next few years,' in Gaia Servadio's words, 'Peppina followed the Requiem Circus led by Verdi and Stolz, between stops at Sant'Agata and Genoa.' The move to the Palazza Doria had exhausted Giuseppina, and meanwhile the fact that 'La' Stolz was earning huge fees added to her sense of betrayal. Verdi's long absences in the company of her rival, who was always booked in the same hotel when the Verdis did manage to go away together, and scurrilous newspaper articles, made her life almost intolerable. She feared that Verdi was about to leave her: to her diary she confided a longing for death to release her from suffering: but such longings were tinged with anxiety that Verdi might bequeath his assets to Stolz instead of to Maria, their adopted daughter.

How well-founded these fears were is difficult to judge. We can only note that, however difficult their relationship, Verdi stayed with Giuseppina and that Teresa Stolz remained a friend of both, ostensibly at least. He may have made a fool of himself in public with a younger woman, but eventually he returned to the management of his estates and contracts. In October 1878 Maria Verdi, their adopted daughter, married Alberto Carrara, the son of a local notary. Her choice of husband pleased both Verdi and Giuseppina, so the quiet family wedding in the chapel at Sant'Agata was a happy occasion for everyone.

The following year, as heavy winter snows melted with the arrival of spring, the river Po burst its banks and flooded the surrounding countryside. Verdi offered a benefit performance of the *Requiem* to raise money for the flood victims. Teresa Stolz and Maria Waldmann came out of retirement to give their services as, in a sense, did Verdi himself. It was a gesture that touched the hearts of the Milanese, who crowded round his hotel after the performance, cheering and shouting *Viva Verdi!* Giuseppina watched from behind a curtain as members of the orchestra of La Scala gathered in the street below to play the overture to *Nabucco*, and the prelude to Act III of *La traviata*.

Dinner the following evening was a private affair with the Ricordis and Francesco Faccio: what took place is best explained by the composer himself in a follow-up letter to his publisher:

You know the origins of this cup of chocolate. You invite me to dine with Faccio. You talk about *Otello*, you talk of Boito. The next day Faccio brings Boito to see me; three days later Boito brings me a sketch of *Otello*. I read it and I like it. I tell him to write the poem; it will always come in handy for him or me or someone else. Now if you come with Boito, I shall be obliged to read the libretto. Either I find it absolutely perfect and you leave it with me – and there I am as good as landed. Or I like it well enough and suggest improvements which Boito accepts – and find myself even more securely hooked. Or I don't like it, and it will be too difficult to tell him so to his face. No, no! You are in too great a hurry.

Verdi suggested that when Boito's libretto was ready it should be posted to him, so that he might consider it quietly and at leisure. The wily old trout was not yet ready to be caught. 'Chocolate' became the code-word for the project. Even these first steps would not have been taken without the tenacity of Giulio Ricordi, who had the wit to realise that Boito was probably the only man who could tempt Verdi out of retirement. His long campaign to achieve a creative partnership between the two men had the support of the Countess Maffei and of Giuseppina, among many others. Although the personalities of the two men were very different they shared certain beliefs. Both were cautious in their dealings with other people; both admired Shakespeare and both believed that composer and librettist were equal partners in creating an opera. Boito put these convictions to the test when he wrote *Mefistofele* to his own verses, an opera that failed badly at its first performance in March 1868 but later attracted much praise.

Ricordi's task had been made no easier by in 1863 when Boito, in his role as a leader of an avant-garde, iconoclastic group, praised a new opera by Faccio and welcomed the restoration of pure Italian art 'on the altar now defiled like the wall of a brothel.' Verdi took this as a personal attack and it needed all Ricordi's tact to smooth ruffled feathers. In 1871 he tried to interest him in *Nerone*, an unfinished work by Boito, but Verdi had refused the bait.

Now, after sixteen years, success appeared to be within Ricordi's grasp. By November, after much suffering on Boito's part – the poor man had to endure the nagging pain of a tooth abscess as well as much bullying from the publisher – his verses were ready. Giuseppina was determined that her husband should be left to make up his own mind: wisely she advised Ricordi to 'let the river find its own way to the sea: it's in the open spaces that certain men are destined to meet and understand one another.'

Other commitments intervened, and it was not until next summer that Verdi was able to examine the text. There was still no commitment on his part: he was much more concerned with the drastic re-working of *Simon Boccanegra*, which he was convinced deserved greater success than it had so far received. Of the many revisions he had in mind the most drastic was an entirely new scene in the Council Chamber. He invited Boito to collaborate, probably to see if they could work together satisfactorily. As we have seen, the poet was unenthusiastic, but set himself to his unwelcome task and produced a masterly piece of theatre which inspired the composer to write some of his finest music to date.

It was then that Boito dropped a disastrous brick. At a banquet given in his honour in Naples he was reported to have said that he had started work on *Otello* unwillingly, but he now found the subject so fascinating that he was sorry not be writing the music himself. When Verdi heard this he was furious, but waited for an explanation. None came, for having made the remark Boito dismissed it from his mind: it simply did not occur to him that it was bound to get back to the composer and that it would cause great offence.

Verdi did not confront Boito directly: instead he wrote to Faccio offering to return the libretto without payment and 'without a shadow of resentment or rancour of any kind.' It was three weeks before this message reached Boito: as soon as it did he wrote Verdi a long letter of apology and explanation:

You alone can set *Otello* to music . . . If I have been able to divine the inherent, powerful musicality of the tragedy, which at first I did not feel, and if I have been to demonstrate it in fact with my libretto, that is because I put myself at the viewpoint of Verdian art . . .

It was a generous letter from a clever man: Boito knew exactly how to touch the composer's pride and appeal to his artistic integrity. In his reply, which was non-committal but civil enough, Verdi suggested that the project should be put to one side for a time. Further delay was a small price to pay for healing the breach, and Boito had the good sense and the good grace to accept it without demur.

It was not until December 1884 that work was resumed. By October 1885 Act IV was complete, waiting to be scored. The great love duet in Act I was ready by March 1886, at which time Verdi started to choose the cast. He went to Paris to engage Victor Maurel as Iago; the title role had long

Cyprus: 15th century. Crowds gather on a quayside in a fierce storm, anxiously awaiting the return of their popular Moorish governor, Otello. He comes safely ashore and announces victory over the Turks. The evil-minded ensign Iago, plots the downfall of his successful rival Cassio by arousing suspicions that he is having an affair with Otello's wife, Desdemona. However, at the end of Act I there is a pure love duet between Otello and Desdemona before Iago's cunning innuendoes reach the ears of the Moor. When they do, the worst fears of the jealous Otello seem to be confirmed when Desdemona is unable to produce a handkerchief he gave her as a love token, Iago having already gathered it up after she had carelessly dropped it. As news comes of his recall to Venice, Otello, mad with rage, strangles Desdemona in her bed. Iago's wife, Emilia, then reveals the full extent of her husband's treachery and Otello kills himself in remorse.

been reserved for Francesco Tamagno, and Romilda Pantaleone was chosen to sing Desdemona.

On 5 November 1886 Giuseppina wrote to the ageing De Sanctis, now almost blind, that 'the last note of *Otello* was written on All Saints' Day. But it was not until a week before Christmas that Verdi told Boito that he had handed the last acts to Garignani, Ricordi's chief copyist. 'Poor Otello! He won't come back here again!' he said. Back came Boito's reply: '*Otello* is. The great dream has become reality!'

Charles Osborne quotes an eye-witness account of the first night:

> From pit to dome, the immense auditorium was one mass of eager faces, sparkling eyes, brilliant toilettes, and splendid jewels. The Italian Court was a rainbow of colours, and Queen Margherita's ladies of honour like a hothouse bouquet of rarest exotics. The first and second tiers of boxes were so packed with the Milanese high-bred women, so covered with dazzling jewels and filmy laces, that the house seemed spanned with a river of light . . .

Among the many critics and composers in the audience were Jules Massenet and Paolo Tosti; sitting in the orchestra, playing second cello was the young Arturo Toscanini; two of the violin desks were occupied by the father and grandfather of Sir John Barbirolli, the much-loved conductor who recorded the opera in 1969 with Dietrich Fischer-Dieskau as Iago. Sir John remembered his father telling him that:

> During rehearsals Verdi had no hesitation in correcting Faccio in regard to any tempo which was not to his liking. Normally rather silent, he would at such moments produce a tremendously loud clicking of his thumb and second finger which resounded throughout the empty theatre and put everyone on the proper course again . . .

As is well known, the character of Iago was of such paramount importance to Verdi that he originally thought of calling the opera by that name. The first Iago was the French baritone Victor Maurel who, although a great singer, must have had what we might call a fragile and therefore at times an unreliable voice. Father used to recall that on certain occasions . . . Maurel would send forth the dread message that he was *senze voce*. Invariably . . . Verdi's reply was the same: 'As long as Maurel can speak I would rather he did Iago than anyone else.'

Victor Maurel (1848-1923), who first sang Iago, is seen here backstage with the composer before the Paris premiere of *Otello*.

After the opening night and the remarkable scenes that followed in the streets of Milan, twenty-four more performances were given at La Scala during the rest of the season. '*Otello* is a masterpiece,' declared Toscanini. 'On your knees, mother, and say *Viva Verdi!*' The resounding success of the opera produced a fresh crop of honours for its composer and enough revenue to make a start on a second cherished project, the building of a rest home in Milan for retired musicians. He had already founded a modest 12-bed hospital which he would not allow to be named after him:

this was built at Villanova to save local people the long journey to Piacenza.

Once the excitement in Milan had died down, Verdi returned to Genoa. In April 1887 Giuseppina underwent surgery for the removal of stomach cysts. Boito, who always asked in his letters that warmest greetings be conveyed to her, showed much concern but was reassured by Verdi, who congratulated him on the 'excellent success of your *Méfistoféles* in France.' The friendship between the two men, forged in the heat of creative endeavour, was a source of comfort and strength to Verdi, who at the age of 73 found that his colleagues and contemporaries were dying off: his librettist Rossi had died in 1885 and his close friend Count Opprandino Arrivabene a year later; Wagner had died four years earlier.

Once again Verdi spent the summer months at Sant'Agata, where Boito was a frequent guest. In November 1887 he took Giuseppina to Genoa and made a number of business trips to Milan and Busseto. In 1889 he tried to discourage celebration of the 50th anniversary of the first performance of *Oberto*: 'this jubilee being extremely disagreeable for me, is neither useful nor practical.' Unknown to Verdi, Boito had been the first to suggest the celebrations and served on the organising committee. He now said that he could not promise 'to scotch the jubilee: the country wants it. But I assure you we will do everything to avoid provoking criticism . . .'

By this time, Verdi had acquired his colleague's taste for musical puzzles: to pass the time he set the text of *Ave Maria* to an 'enigmatic scale' devised by Adolfo Crescentini, professor of music at Bologna. 'Another *Ave Maria*!' he wrote to Boito. 'It will be my fourth! In this way I could hope, after my death, to be beatified by the Holy Father!' to which Boito replied that he would need to write a good many more Ave Marias to make up for Iago's creed in *Otello*. The *Ave Maria*, unlike a setting of the *Pater Noster* he composed in 1880, became part of his last published work, the *Four Sacred Pieces* for four-part chorus and orchestra (1898).

In May 1889 and again in late June Verdi met Boito in Milan, and in the course of conversation let slip – not for the first time – that he had long thought of writing a comic opera. This time the quick-witted Boito refused to let it pass, and suggested *Falstaff* as a subject and in a few hours produced a rough outline. 'Excellent! Excellent!' wrote Verdi the following day. 'Before reading your sketch I chose to re-read the *Merry Wives*, the two parts of *Henry IV* and *Henry V*; and I can only repeat *excellent*, for it would be impossible to do better than you have done.' To read four Shakespeare plays and a scenario in one day, and then comment in detail on them, is a task that would daunt most of us: for a man in his mid-seventies, if true, it is an astonishing feat.

Twenty-four hours later doubts set in. 'As long as we roam the world of ideas everything smiles on us,' he wrote to Boito. 'But once we come to earth and face practical questions, doubts and discouragement arise. In outlining *Falstaff* have you ever thought of the enormous number of my years? . . . what if the effort were too much for me? And what if I did not manage to finish the music?' Verdi was haunted by the thought that by distracting Boito from *Nerone* he would be blamed for the delay and that 'the thunderbolts of public malice would fall upon my shoulders.'

He need not have worried, for the massive opera on the life of Nero

Placido Domingo as Otello at the Royal Opera House, Covent Garden, in 1992.

was never finished, even though Boito worked on it for forty years. He hastened to reassure the composer:

> The fact is that I never think of your age either when I speak with you, or when I write to you, or when I work for you . . . Tragedy makes the person writing it actually *suffer* . . . but the joking of laughter and comedy exhilarate mind and body. 'A smile adds a thread to the fabric of life.' I do not know if this is the exact wording . . . but it is certainly a truth. . . . There is only one way to end better than with *Otello* and that is to end victoriously with *Falstaff*. After having made all the cries and lamentations of the human heart resound, to end with an immense outburst of hilarity! It's dazzling!
> . . . I have told no one. If we work in secret we will work in peace. I await your decision which, as is your custom, will be free and resolute. I must not influence it. Your decision will in any event be wise and strong, whether you say *Enough*, or you say *Again*.
> Yours affectionately,
> A. Boito

'Amen; and so be it!' came the reply. The truth is, of course, that only death could have stopped Verdi writing *Falstaff*. The perceptive Boito said a few weeks later that Giuseppina knew that a new opera was in the making: on one occasion he sent 'many greetings to Giuseppina, the prophetess.'

Then follows a sequence of letters, some dealing with details in the text and others that reveal a growing concern about the failing health of their mutual friend Faccio. In May 1890 Boito became honorary director of the Parma Conservatory, in effect to stand in for Faccio while he was away on sick leave.

This news was warmly welcomed by Verdi in a letter dated 23 May 1890 in which he confesses that he has 'done nothing on "Big Belly", but we will talk about him at Sant'Agata'. In November of that year yet another friend, Giuseppe Piroli, died in Rome, to be followed by Emanuele Muzio soon afterwards in Paris. Both men were born in Busseto.

Months passed without further progress: 'I still haven't been able to warm up the engine!' wrote Verdi in March 1891. But his enthusiasm for the venture remained intense, as these extracts from a letter to Gino Monaldi show:

I've wanted to write a comic opera for forty years, and I've known *The Merry Wives of Windsor* for fifty . . .

Now Boito . . . has written me a lyric comedy quite unlike any other. I'm enjoying myself writing the music; without plans of any sort and I don't even know if I'll finish it . . . I'm enjoying myself. Falstaff is a rogue who gets up to every kind of mischief . . . but in an amusing way. He's a *type* . . .

Later, in June 1891, he confirmed in an interview published in the *Gazzetta musicale* that he was still working on the opera but had no definite date in mind for its completion. He told Giulio Ricordi, even at this late stage, that he was writing the opera in order 'to pass the time' and that no useful purpose would be served 'in making plans or accepting terms, however loosely worded':

When I was young, even if I felt under the weather I could stay at my desk for up to ten hours at a stretch . . . and more than once I would begin work at four o'clock in the morning and go on until four o'clock in the afternoon with only a cup of coffee to keep me going . . . working continually without stopping to take breath. Now I can't.

Verdi's refusal to be tied down was partly the act of a prudent old man aware that he might not be able to complete his task. And he had not lost his wicked delight in keeping friends guessing and pulling wool over the eyes of the press.

The death of Faccio in July was a great sorrow to composer and librettist, and they did no further work for several weeks. In October a rumour that the opera was ready had to be scotched by Ricordi. In the New Year, Verdi, Giuseppina and Boito all suffered from influenza, but when the exchange of letters was resumed, it dealt more with costumes and matters concerning the production than with the music or the libretto.

Other concerns intervened. Prompted by an article in the press, Verdi wrote to Boito in August 1892 to 'work night and day if necessary to see that *Nerone* is ready next year. Indeed, at this moment you should have the news published 'This year at La Scala, *Falstaff*; next year, *Nerone*. If I have spoken out of turn, if I have said too much . . . consider it all unsaid.'

Later in the month, in a reference to *Falstaff*, frustration creeps in: 'I write and work like a dog, but I never finish it.' In fact, his task was almost completed. From the end of September 1892 there is a break in the correspondence because the Verdis and Boito saw each other virtually every day. Boito toiled alone on translations, but he also spent much time with Verdi putting the finishing touches to their work, correcting proofs and preparing for rehearsals due to start in the New Year. Verdi and Giuseppina arrived in Milan on 4 January 1893: the eighty-year-old composer took charge, working six to eight hours a day.

A sudden crisis arose during the preparations for the opening night when Victor Maurel, under contract for the title role, demanded higher fees and a monopoly in the part itself. He under-estimated his man, for even in old age Verdi had lost none of his negotiating skill or tenacity. He promptly threatened to withdraw *Falstaff* from La Scala, which he had always considered too large a venue for the work, or so he said. Maurel climbed down, a compromise was reached and rehearsals went ahead.

The first performance of *Falstaff* was more like a state occasion than the opening night of a new opera. Government ministers and officials were present with their wives, together with publishers and writers, international and local music critics, younger composers, including Puccini and Mascagni, and artists, among whom was Giovanni Boldoni, who painted the best-known portrait of the composer.

The performance was a triumph. Verdi took many curtain calls, insisting that Boito should stand with him on stage to share the applause. As before, huge crowds gathered round the stage door and under the

Donald Maxwell as Falstaff and Suzanne Murphy as Alice Ford in the Welsh National Opera production of *Falstaff* in 1988.

balcony of his hotel room, but on this occasion the members of the orchestra who had also gathered there were asked not to play: the Maestro needed to rest. The following day messages of goodwill and congratulation were received from all over the world. There came a rumour that he was to be created Marquis of Busseto, a prospect that so appalled him that he appealed to the Minister of Education to nip any such proposal in the bud.

That the critics should have been unanimous in their praise was to be expected, but the enthusiasm of the audience – once the sense of great occasion had started to wane – was less secure. Some opera-goers were puzzled by the new work. Where had the great tunes gone – the kind that errand boys used to whistle in the street? There were few enough in *Otello*, but in *Falstaff* there were none. Had Verdi's melodic powers deserted him at last? Where were the rousing choruses, the graceful cabalettas and the powerful contrasts and climaxes?

These were the questions asked by some members of those early audiences, who were puzzled by what they had heard. There is an inexhaustible energy about the music and an endless flow of ideas that tumble over each with such rapidity that on first hearing it is easy to miss what is happening. There simply is no time for set arias with their preparatory recitatives. The wit, the humour, the gentle irony, the wealth of incident and all the other ingredients in Boito's brilliant libretto are picked up and

reflected in music wrought with such delicacy, and with so light a touch, that from start to finish it sparkles, dances and races along like quicksilver. 'That the mechanical commonplaces of 1848 should have been fanned into such magnificent life forty-five years later,' writes Julian Budden, 'is a miracle of regeneration difficult to parallel in the history of music.'

Regeneration, certainly – how else can so astonishing an achievement for a man in his eighties be explained? But the continuity is there as well because despite the stylistic gaps that undoubtedly exist between *Aida* and *Otello* on the one hand and, even more markedly, between *Otello* and *Falstaff* on the other, it is still possible to discern an unbroken line in Verdi's creative life that links, in a single triumphal arch, the *bel canto* traditions of Donizetti and Rossini with the dramatic realism of the modern operatic stage.

When Verdi was born, Schubert was just setting out on his career and Beethoven's 7th Symphony was first heard in public. At the time of his death, Elgar and Sibelius had already made their mark, Schoenberg had written *Verklärte Nacht* and the seventeen-year-old Stravinsky was waiting in the wings. Such comparisons are tempting and far too much can be read into them, but they do enable us to place the life of Verdi in its chronological setting and they do reveal its remarkable compass. When we consider the span of that triumphal arch and the scale of his artistic achievement we can only gaze in silent awe and gratitude.

If this book were an opera it would end at this point, with the cheers of the La Scala audience ringing in the old man's ears. But life is a messy, untidy business. That's why we need Art to give it form and meaning. That's why, like Verdi, we sometimes need to invent reality. He knew, of course, that *Falstaff* was his last adventure. 'Do you remember the third evening?' he asks in a letter to the soprano Emma Zilli, who sang Nannetta:

> I said my farewell to you all, and you were all a little moved . . . Imagine what that farewell was for me. It meant, 'We shall never meet again as artists' . . . It's all over! . . . You are fortunate to have so much of your career ahead of you, and I wish that it may always be as splendid for you as you deserve.

The flames subsided but the embers glowed: it must not be imagined that after *Falstaff* the Maestro put down his pen and waited patiently for the end. There were still plenty of musical and business affairs to occupy his time and his mind. In September 1893 the faithful Boito suggested that 'we must think of another work to do together because otherwise we, who do not like pointless letters, will end up writing to each other once in a blue moon.' Not long afterwards, Peppina had let slip an incautious remark, possibly to do with his unmarried state, and to the apology Boito sent this simple reply:

> So I thank you very much, dear Maestro, for your good letter; and Signora Peppina must not beat her breast. We were born, the three of us, to understand one another very well even when our words are unfaithful to our thoughts.

In September 1894 Verdi and Giuseppina visited Paris for the last time.

One of the last portraits of Giuseppina Strepponi.

He was there to supervise a production of *Otello*, for which he had written a ballet. The President of the Republic invited him to his box, and before presenting him to the audience told Verdi that he had been awarded the Grand Cross of the *Légion d'Honneur*. A few days later, together with Ambroise Thomas, he attended a memorial service for Gounod at the Madeleine, which was followed by a State Banquet at the Elysée Palace. Giuseppina was among the guests of honour, one imagines to her considerable satisfaction, as she had been ignored in Rome on a similar occasion at a dinner given in her husband's honour by the King of Italy.

On their return to Sant'Agata, Verdi turned his thoughts again to the proposed *Casa di Riposa per Musicisti* in Milan. The architect Camillo Boito, Arrigo's elder brother, was commissioned to draw up plans for a rest home on two storeys, providing accommodation for one hundred professional musicians who had no pension or other means of support.

He also took up his last published work, the *Four Sacred Pieces*. He had never intended that they should be played together, but to the earlier *Ave Maria* based on the enigmatic scale he added a *Stabat Mater*, a *Laudi alla Vergine Maria* to verses from the last stanza of Dante's *Paradiso*, and a magnificent setting of the *Te Deum*, his last composition of any substance.

Verdi's letters to Boito reveal that he made further revisions to his work a year later. By that time, October 1894, other priorities took precedence

because Giuseppina, whose health had been poor for some time,
contracted pneumonia on the eve of their planned departure to Genoa for
the winter season. As she went into a decline Verdi was at her side for
hours at a time. He gathered a bunch of the last of the season's violets for
her, but she could not smell them: a few days later she died.

After a simple funeral service in Busseto her body was taken to Milan
for burial. Verdi was reduced to silence, as he wrote to a friend:

> Great loss does not demand great expression: it asks for silence, iso-
> lation, I would say even the torture of reflection. There is something
> superficial about all outward show: it is a profanity.

He was supported in his grief by his friends including Teresa Stolz, now
a constant companion, by Boito who visited him as often as he could, by
the loyal Ricordis and by Maria Carrara-Verdi and her family. Boito had
persuaded Verdi to allow three of the *Four Sacred Pieces* to be performed
in Paris: he had intended to attend the concert in person but his doctors
advised against the journey after he had suffered a series of minor heart
attacks. He asked Boito to take his place, and true to his old form, issued a
stream of performance notes and instructions.

The affairs of the outside world, in which he continued to take a lively
interest, touched him directly for the last time in July 1900, when King
Umberto was assassinated by an anarchist. The widowed Queen wrote a
prayer which was published in the press, and there were many who
suggested that Verdi should be asked to set it to music. He declined, but
was moved to sketch out a few bars, found later among his papers.

He was variable in mood, as he had been all his life. Teresa Stolz told
Maria Waldmann, now a grandmother, that:

> Our beloved Maestro is well, despite his eighty-seven years. He
> enjoys a good appetite, sleeps well, often goes out for drives, some-
> times walks a little, but complains of his legs, saying that he would
> take longer walks but that his legs are weak.

At other times he was less buoyant: 'Why am I still in this world?' he
asked. In December he moved to the comfort of his suite in Milan's Grand
Hotel, where he spent an increasing amount of time to be nearer his
friends. Christmas and the New Year were spent in their company, and all
congratulated him on his vigour and good health.

But on 21 January 1901 there came the answer to the unanswered
question. As Verdi sat on his bed, buttoning a waistcoat, he suffered a
stroke which left him unconscious. He survived for several days, while his
friends and the world waited for news. Black drapes were hung from the
walls of the Grand Hotel, and straw was laid on the cobbled street outside
to muffle the sound of passing carriages and other horse-drawn traffic. He
died in silence, without recovering consciousness, at ten minutes to three
on the morning of 27 January 1901.

'Verdi is dead', Boito wrote later to Bellaigue. 'He has taken away with
him an enormous amount of light and of vital warmth; we were all
brightened by the sunshine of that Olympian old age'. The letter continues:

> He died magnificently, like a formidable, silenced fighter . . . His
> head bowed on his chest, his eyebrows stern, he looked down and

The scene in the Piazzale Cairoli, Milan, as the two coffins were carried in procession to their final resting place.

seemed to measure with his gaze an unknown and formidable adversary, and to calculate mentally the strength required to oppose him. He also put up a heroic resistance . . . poor Maestro! How good and beautiful he was to the very end . . . but never before have I experienced such a feeling of hatred against death, of contempt for that mysterious, blind, stupid, triumphant and craven power. It needed the death of this octogenarian to arouse these feelings in me.

Plans had been drawn up for a magnificent public funeral, but when it was found that Verdi had left strict instructions that it should be a modest affair, these were abandoned and he was quietly laid to rest beside his wife in the municipal cemetery of Milan. His final wish was that they should be moved to the *Casa di Riposa* as soon the building was ready, and a month later this instruction was carried out. The two coffins were taken through the city's crowded streets in a slow-moving procession, followed by Italian royal princes, leading politicians and other public figures from all parts of the country and abroad. As they passed, many people in the crowd softly sang *Va, pensiero*, the sound of which reached a crescendo at the gates where a choir of eight hundred stood waiting to sing the chorus in full voice.

They were conducted by Arturo Toscanini.

A new century had dawned.

Selected Bibliography

Amis, John; Rose, Michael, *Words About Music*, Faber & Faber (London: 1989)

Anderson, James, *Dictionary of Opera and Operetta*, (Columbia Marketing: 1989)

Beecham, Sir Thomas, *A Mingled Chime*, Hutchinson & Co. Ltd (London: 1944)

Bonavia, Ferruccio, *Verdi*, Oxford University Press (Oxford: 1930)

Budden, Julian, *Verdi* (The Master Musicians), J. M. Dent & Sons (London: 1985)

Budden, Julian, *The Operas of Verdi* (3 vols), Cassells (London: 1981 (rev. ed. O.U.P. 1992))

Conari, Marcello & Medici, Mario, (Eng. ed. W. Weaver),*The Verdi-Boito Correspondence*, The Univ. of Chicago Press (Chicago/London: 1994)

Dent, Edward J. Opera: *The Musical Companion* (ed. A. L. Bacharach) Book III, Victor Gollancz Ltd (London: 1934)

Dent, Edward J. *Opera*, Penguin Books (London 1940)

Douglas, Nigel, *Legendary Voices*, André Deutsch (London: 1992)

Douglas, Nigel, *More Legendary Voices*, André Deutsch (London: 1994)

Gobbi, Tito, *World of Italian Opera*, Hamish Hamilton Ltd (London: 1984)

Headington, Christopher; Westbrook, Roy; Barfoot, Terry, *Opera – A History*, The Bodley Head (London: 1987)

Hopkins, Antony, *Music All Around Me*, Leslie Frewin (London: 1967)

Hussey, Dyneley, *Verdi* (The Master Musicians), J. M. Dent & Sons (London: 1948)

Lebrecht, Norman, *The Book of Musical Anecdotes*, Andre Deutsch (London: 1985)

Martin, George, *Aspects of Verdi*, Robson Books (London: 1988)

Matthews, Denis, *In Pursuit of Music*, Victor Gollancz Ltd (London: 1966)

Matthews, Denis, *Arturo Toscanini*, Midas Books (Tunbridge Wells: 1982)

Osborne, Charles, *The Complete Operas of Verdi*, Victor Gollancz Ltd (London: 1988)

Osborne, Charles, *Letters of Giuseppe Verdi*, Victor Gollancz Ltd (London: 1971)

Osborne, Charles, *Verdi*, Macmillan London Limited (1978)

Parker, Roger (ed.), *The Oxford Illustrated History of Opera*, Oxford University Press (Oxford: 1994)

Rosenthal, Harold and Warrack, John (eds.) *The Concise Oxford Dictionary of Opera*, Oxford University Press (Oxford: 1980)

Rosselli, John, *Music and Musicians in 19th Century Italy*, Batsford (London: 1991)

Sachs, Harvey, *Toscanini*, Weidenfeld & Nicholson (London: 1978)

Sachs, Harvey, *Reflections on Toscanini*, Robson Books (London: 1992)

Servadio, Gaia, *The Real Traviata*, Hodder and Stoughton (London: 1994)

Slonimsky, Nicolas, *Lexicon of Musical Invective*, University of Washington Press (Seattle and London: 1953)

Southwell-Sander, Peter, *Verdi: His Life and Times*, Midas Books (Tunbridge Wells: 1978)

Swanston, Hamish E.G., *In Defence of Opera*, Penguin Books (London: 1978)

Toye, Francis, *Verdi: Lives of the Great Composers* (ed. A. L. Bacharach) Penguin Books (London 1943)

Toye, Francis, *Verdi: His Life and Works*, Victor Gollancz (London: 1931)

Werfel, Franz, *Verdi, A Novel of the Opera*, Allen, Towne and Heath Inc. (New York: 1947)

Whittall, Arnold, *Romantic Music*, Thames and Hudson (London: 1987)

Williams, Stephen, *Come to the Opera*, Hutchinson & Co. Ltd, (London: 1948)

Many titles in the 'Opera Guides' published by John Calder in London and the Riverrun Press in New York, in association with English National Opera and the Royal Opera, are an invaluable source of information and comment on the operas of Verdi, as are relevant articles in the annual programmes issued by Glyndebourne Festival Opera.

Index

CREDITS

Picture research by
Image Select:
Elizabeth Davis
Alexander Goldberg

Picture credits
Clive Barda: p. 99
Hulton-Deutsch: pp. 97, 115, 149
Zoë Dominic: p. 151
Mary Evans Picture Library: p. 39
Image Select: pp. 1, 9, 10, 13, 17, 23, 27, 29, 30, 31, 33, 36, 37, 41, 44, 47, 53, 55, 68, 69, 95, 109, 117, 127, 129, 131, 135, 136, 139, 140-141, 145, 147, 155, 156
Popperphoto: pp. 48, 57, 75, 79, 93, 107, 121
Ann Ronan at Image Select: pp. 45, 59, 65, 85

The publishers wish to thank those authors, translators and their publishers for permission to quote brief extracts verbatim where appropriate. Every effort has been made to trace copyright owners but it is possible that not all have been identified. If so, the publishers would be glad to receive details so that acknowledgement can be made in future editions.